BASIS FOR BUSINESS
WORKBOOK

B2

MINDY EHRHART KRULL

ADVISERS
ANNE HODGSON, BERLIN
KATHRYN NUSSDORF, BERLIN

Basis for Business B2
Workbook mit Audio-CD

Im Auftrag des Verlages erarbeitet von	Mindy Ehrhart Krull, Dresden
Beratende Mitarbeit	Anne Hodgson, Berlin
	Kathryn Nussdorf, Berlin
Redaktion	Stacy Dorgan Bentz
Redaktionelle Mitarbeit	Katrina Walsh
Bildredaktion	Uta Hübner
Projektkoordination	Anna Batrla
Projektleitung	Murdo MacPhail
Umschlaggestaltung	hawemannundmosch, bureau für konzeption und gestaltung, Berlin
Layout und technische Umsetzung	Sabine Theuring, Berlin
Cover	© Shutterstock, Yuri Arcurs

Bildquellen
S. 10 © iStockphoto, Troels Graugaard; S. 17 © iStockphoto, Mark Bowden; S. 26 © iStockphoto, AIMSTOCK; S. 32 © iStockphoto, Aldo Murillo; S. 39 © iStockphoto, Abel Mitja Varela; S. 51 © iStockphoto, Stigur Karlsson; S. 57 © iStockphoto, mediaphotos

Weitere Kursmaterialien
Coursebook mit Audio-CDs und Phrasebook   ISBN 978-3-06-521008-9
Teaching Guide mit Toolbox CD-ROM   ISBN 978-3-06-521010-2

www.cornelsen.de

1. Auflage, 2. Druck 2017

© 2012 Cornelsen Schulverlage GmbH, Berlin
© 2017 Cornelsen Verlag GmbH, Berlin

Druck: H. Heenemann, Berlin

ISBN 978-3-06-521009-6

PEFC zertifiziert
Dieses Produkt stammt aus nachhaltig bewirtschafteten Wäldern und kontrollierten Quellen.
www.pefc.de
PEFC/04-31-1156

Table of contents

Das **Basis for Business B2** *Workbook* hilft Ihnen, Ihre Englischkenntnisse selbstständig zu erweitern. Durch das handliche Pocket-Format kann Sie das *Workbook* überall begleiten: Auf dem Weg zur Arbeit, auf Geschäftsreisen, in einer Kaffeepause oder am Schreibtisch.

Die abwechslungsreichen Übungen im *Workbook* erweitern und vertiefen die im Kursbuch **Basis for Business B2** behandelten Themen und Strukturen. Das *Workbook* kann dabei sowohl zum Selbststudium zu Hause als auch im Unterricht verwendet werden.

Das **Basis for Business B2** *Workbook* ist in zehn *Units* unterteilt, die auf das Kursbuch abgestimmt sind. Sie enthalten:
* Übungen zu den wichtigsten Grammatikstrukturen und zum Wortschatz
* *Over to you*-Übungen, um das Gelernte zu personalisieren
* sprachliche Tipps und *Did you know?*-Kästen mit ergänzenden Informationen zum Thema der Unit
* 3 *Progress checks* zur Selbsteinschätzung und Überprüfung der Lernfortschritte
* Hörverständnisübungen in jeder *Unit* (Audio-CD)
* vollständige Transkripte und Lösungen (im Anhang)

Wir wünschen Ihnen mit dem **Basis for Business B2** *Workbook* viel Spaß und Erfolg!

Introductions

1

1 Listen to the speaker. For each pair of words, circle the form of the verb you hear.

Unit checklist
- introduce yourself and your company
- talk about roles and responsibilities
- describe company structures and processes
- read about real company management structures

1 provides / is providing

2 look / are looking

3 includes / is including

4 aim / are aiming

5 do research / are doing research

6 increase / are increasing

Tip "Keynote" refers to the main speech at a conference or event. It is usually given by a special guest and deals with the main theme of the event. "Keynote" can be used alone as a noun but is more often seen as an adjective: keynote speaker
keynote speech (also called a keynote address)

2 Which signal words or phrases in the box are often used with the simple present and which are used with the present continuous? Complete the table.

every day · at the moment · always · usually · currently · sometimes · at present · right now

Simple present	Present continuous

3 You are the keynote speaker at a conference. Use at least five of the verbs in the box to write a short introduction about yourself and your company that uses both the simple present and present continuous. Use some signal words and phrases from exercise 2.

work • live • prepare • specialize in • deal with • open • launch • have • coordinate • make • provide • do

. . . .

. . . .

. . . .

. . . .

. . . .

4 Listen to four short conversations. For each, write down the question tag or echo of information used to keep the conversation going. In one conversation, there is one of each.

1 . . . .

2 . . . .

3 . . . .

4 . . . .

5 Choose the correct ending or response for each of the sentences often used at conferences and in introductions.

1 It's nice to …
  a   meet you again.
  b   see you again.

2 Maybe we'll see …
  a   each other later.
  b   us later.

3 How do you do?
  a   How do you do?
  b   I'm fine, thanks.

4 I wanted to ask you, …
  a   do you see often Isabel?
  b   do you often see Isabel?

5 What …
  a   makes your firm?
  b   does your firm make?

6 We heard your company …
  a   is restructuring.
  b   restructures.

6 Complete the sentences in the email with the prepositions from the box. Then underline the collocations that are formed with the prepositions.

on • for • to • in • of • at • for • to • with

From: Ruth Simmons
To: Derrick Evans
Cc:
Subject: Job opening for factory manager

Dear Mr Evans

It was nice meeting you . . . . . .[1] the conference. As I said when we met, right now I am filling in . . . . . .[2] a colleague who is . . . . . .[3] leave. He is in charge . . . . . .[4] the construction of a large factory in the Czech Republic. We are looking for a new factory manager, and I thought you might be perfect . . . . . .[5] the job. The manager will work closely . . . . . .[6] me as well as the production team. He/she reports . . . . . .[7] me, and I report . . . . . .[8] the Chief Operating Officer.

Please let me know if you are interested . . . . . .[9] the job or if you would like more details.

Best wishes
Ruth Simmons

7 Complete the sentences with the correct forms of the verbs in brackets (simple present or present continuous active or passive).

1 **A:** The coffee is excellent today! Who made it?

   B: Well, usually the coffee . . . . (make) by Herb, but Greta

   . . . . (make) it this week since Herb is on holiday.

2 **A:** The database . . . . (update) on a regular basis, right?

   B: Yes, but no one has updated it since Michaela went on maternity leave.

3 **A:** Where is Dara?

   B: In Cape Town. She . . . . (attend) a trade fair this week.

4 **A:** How are preparations coming along for the meeting with the new client?

   B: Everything is fine. The presentation . . . . (prepare) by our marketing team. Kelly has distributed information to all employees. We

   . . . . (feel) certain that the meeting will be a success.

8 As part of her job at a chocolate manufacturer, Tara explains the process of making chocolate to guests at the visitors' centre. Complete her text using the simple present passive or present continuous passive.

Good morning and thank you for joining me for a tour today. Our company has been making chocolate bars and other chocolate products since 1898. Today I'm going to show you how chocolate . . . . .¹ (make).

Please follow me. Our first room shows where cocoa comes from. As you can see on the map, the fruit that . . . . .² (use) to make chocolate grows on cacao trees in South America, Asia and Africa. Here's a picture of the cacao tree. The fruit that grows on the trees is called a cacao pod, and the seeds of the cacao pod are what we call cocoa beans. Please look at the movie behind me. Large cacao pods . . . . .³ (open) by some of our employees in Africa.

Now please come with me to what we call "the roasting room". After the beans . . . . .⁴ (clean), they are sorted and roasted. The machine you can see through the window is an example of a roasting machine. After the beans are roasted, the inner part of the beans . . . . .⁵ (remove). This is the part of the bean that is used to make chocolate.

Please follow me to the last room. Look through the window to your right. See the machine operating? The beans . . . . .⁶ (make) into chocolate liquor. Then, additional ingredients such as milk and cocoa butter . . . . .⁷ (add) to the liquor and cooked to make the sweet, creamy chocolate we all love.

On your left you can see a few of our employees. The hot combination . . . . .⁸ (put) into metal frames we call molds. Now let's move on …

9 **Match the words from the two boxes to form collocations. Then use the collocations to complete the sentences.**

1	hierarchical	a	approach
2	hands-on	b	responsibility
3	inventory	c	costs
4	flexible	d	management
5	individual	e	structure
6	production	f	structure

1 You could say that our company has a traditional . . . .
Employees are not involved in decision-making processes and there's a lot of
bureaucracy.

2 Our open corporate culture and flat hierarchy ensures that employees have
high degrees of . . . .

3 I like our . . . ., but sometimes it takes a long time for
decisions to be made.

4 Our factories were just modernized, so we hope we can reduce our
. . . . by one-third next year.

5 Last year our biggest challenge was . . . . As a result,
we upgraded the computer systems in all warehouses.

6 Our manager wants us to use a . . . . When he hires a
new employee, a person's experience on the job is much more important to
him than academic qualifications.

10 **Write the sentences you hear. The sentences describe one company from pages 16–17 in the coursebook. Which is it?**

. . . .

. . . .

. . . .

. . . .

11 **Complete the chart with the correct word forms.**

Noun	Verb	Adjective
bureaucracy		1
2	to compensate	compensatory
corporation		3
flexibility		4
independence		5
6	to initiate	initial
production	to produce	7
rank/ranking	8	

12 **In 5–6 sentences, describe your company using as many words from exercise 11 as possible.**

Over to you

My company offers its employees excellent compensation and flexible work hours.

It's ranked as the most family-friendly company in the region.

. . . .

. . . .

. . . .

. . . .

. . . .

1 Which words or phrases in the box are used in formal emails and which are used in informal emails? Complete the table. Then draw a line to connect the words or phrases in the formal emails column with the words or phrases in the informal emails column that have the same meaning.

> I can't make it • with reference to • sorry again • it's about • please accept my apologies • because of • I'm sorry, but • I will be unable to attend • Dear • due to • I regret to inform you • Hi

Formal emails	Informal emails

2 Choose the correct words to complete the email. Is the email formal or informal? How can you tell?

From: Sabine Williams
To: Frank Forrest
Cc:
Subject: A good restaurant

Hi Frank

I got your message and I think that the best place to take the consultants for lunch is Fishy Business, a fish restaurant located on 15th Street. It is/'s been¹ there for/since² 30 years. Our employees go/have been going³ there for lunch for/since⁴ 2008, when our offices moved to the city. We took/have taken⁵ a few clients there for four weeks/four weeks ago⁶. They absolutely loved it.

I was there for lunch for two days/two days ago⁷ and ordered/have ordered⁸ my favorite entree (shrimp scampi). It was/has been⁹ better than ever!

The restaurant is offering/has been offering¹⁰ vegetarian (non-fish) dishes for/since¹¹ 2010, so you don't have to worry if someone in the group doesn't eat meat.
You weren't/haven't been¹² working here then, but last December we had/have had¹³ our company holiday party at the restaurant.

Definitely make a reservation. Sometimes it gets/has gotten¹⁴ very busy, even at lunch!

Best
Sabine

3 Read the sales flyer. Form questions to match the answers.

HideAway Inc.

Twenty years ago, you didn't have to worry about your online image.

But things have changed.

Information – even your personal data – is everywhere.

That's where we can help. At HideAway, we've been managing online information for people since 2011. We've helped film stars, famous politicians and top business leaders change their images and their lives.

How do we do it? We analyse the online information about you. Then you decide what stays and what goes.

Do a search of your name online, and don't forget to check for pictures. Then call us.

You need us because online information doesn't have to be permanent.

1 . . . .

No, you didn't.

2 . . . .

Information, even your personal data.

3 . . . .

Since 2011.

4 . . . .

Film stars, politicians and top business leaders.

5 . . . .

You do.

6 . . . .

Because online information doesn't have to be permanent.

Did you know?

When you apply for a job, a positive online reputation is important: a 2010 study found that 86 per cent of employers considered an applicant's online reputation before making a decision about who to hire (Time.com, 2011).

4 The marketing manager at Designed by You wants to make some changes to the company profile on the Internet. Change the sentences to simple present passive or simple past passive. (Tip: use words such as *the company* as an alternative to repeating the company's name.)

○ ○ ○   Designed by You

◄ ►   +   ⊖ http://www.designedbyyou.com/   ¢   (Q▾

▥ ▦

About us: Designed by You

Fashion students Samantha Richards and Kara Mendez founded Designed by You in 2009.

. . . . ¹

The website allows customers to design their own clothing online. After the customers create their designs, they enter their body measurements into the website. Designed by You makes the clothing. . . . . ²

Then, Designed by You sends the clothing to the customer. . . . .

. . . . ³

Because the website was such a big success, Designed by You opened its first store in California in 2011. . . . . ⁴

In 2012, Designed by You expanded the original website. . . . .

. . . . ⁵ Now customers can use the online system to create their own clothing lines. Designed by You markets the clothing lines to different clothing stores.

. . . . ⁶

---

5 Match the words or phrases (1–6) to their definitions (a–e) when used in small talk. One definition must be used twice.

1	anyway	**a**		to be very honest
2	whereabouts	**b**		to introduce a question that may or may not be related to the topic being discussed
3	speaking of (which)	**c**		to add a statement not related to the current topic / change the subject
4	quite frankly	**d**		to say or ask something related to the topic being discussed but not related to the last statement
5	so	**e**		where or approximately where
6	by the way			

6 Add a sentence of more information to each answer. Then write a follow-up question for each that you could use to hand the conversations over to a partner to keep them flowing.

Tip Beware of a false friend! In German, "so" is often used at the beginning of a sentence to mean "therefore" or "thus". "So" does not function this way in English, especially in written English. Use "therefore" or "thus" instead.

1 A: How long have you lived in Bonn?
   B: Six years. . . . .

2 A: So, how many employees work at your firm?
   B: About 75. . . . .

3 A: I'm so glad we got a sunny day for the party.
   B: Me, too. . . . .

4 A: Well, the keynote speaker should be good. Have you ever heard him before? He's an excellent speaker.
   B: No, I haven't. . . . .

5 A: Oh, I see you ordered the steak. How is it?
   B: It's very good, thank you. . . . .

6 A: I just returned from Munich. I was there for a big football game. What about you? Are you a football fan?
   B: No, actually I'm not. . . . .

7 Two business partners meet for the first time and make small talk before ordering their food. Put the conversation in order.

Ulrike

1 Good morning, you must be Tamara.

   Well, during business meetings I always order the English breakfast.

   What are you planning to see while you're here?

   Nice to meet you, too. Did you have any trouble finding the restaurant?

   So, have you been to Köln before?

   I guess we should try to order right away. It can get very busy here.

   It's great that the weather is a little warmer today.

   Well, I'd start by … Oh, here comes the waiter for our order.

Tamara

   Sounds great. I'll have the English breakfast and a large black coffee.

   No, this is my first visit. Well, this is the first visit during which I'll have time to look around.

   Really? Well then, I'll have to consider myself lucky.

   Ulrike, good morning. It's a pleasure to meet you in person.

   I'm not sure. What do you recommend?

   None at all, thanks for asking. It is very conveniently located.

   Good idea. Do you have any suggestions?

5 Listen to check your answers.

8 Two former colleagues see each other at a train station. Start in box 1. Choose response a or b. Follow the instructions. In your opinion, what is the path of the most successful conversation?

Tom: Oh, hi Sam, it's nice to see you again.
a Hello Tom, it's been a long time since we've seen each other. Almost two years? How have you been? **Go to 2.**
b Hello Tom, how are you? It's good to see you. Are you coming or going? **Go to 6.**

Tom: Well, I'm based in London now, so life is always interesting. And what about you?
a Oh, I'm still based in Hamburg. Do you still travel a lot for work? London is the perfect portal to all parts of the world. **Go to 3.**
b Oh, I'm still based in Hamburg. So, how are things working out at your new firm? **Go to 7.**

Tom: Well, actually I've just returned from a business trip to Mexico. It was a successful trip but I missed the big game!
a Mexico, really? What were you doing there? **Go to 9.**
b Oh, don't worry about the game. It was clear who was going to win after the first 15 minutes. By the way, what part of Mexico were you in? **Go to 4.**

Tom: Well, I had a few business meetings in Mexico City. My girlfriend came along, so after the meetings we had our holidays in Cancún. Have you ever been there?
a No, I'm afraid not, but it's on our list of places we hope to see someday. Do you recommend a visit? **Go to 5.**
b No, I haven't. We've heard too many news reports about illness due to the water. You know, I think they call it "Montezuma's revenge". **Go to 9.**

Tom: Yes, I do. It's absolutely beautiful and the people are very friendly and helpful. Anyway, sorry for the business talk, but I heard that your company just bought a top competitor?
a Yes, that's right. It was an excellent decision. **Go to 9.**
b Well, you heard correct. We've acquired TWR Inc. It seemed like the right time. Speaking of which, how are things at your company? **Go to 7.**

Tom: Things are going well, thanks. The company is restructuring, so it's a little unclear what the organization will look like in a year or two. Basically, we're going from a hierarchical structure to a matrix structure. Both have advantages and disadvantages.
a Yes, of course. **Go to 9.**
b Really? I wasn't aware of that. Well, I'm sure there would be a job for you with us if you ever wanted to come back. I'd love the opportunity to work with you again. **Go to 8.**

Tom: Oh, I have a few meetings in the city today. Are you by any chance staying in the city tonight? Maybe we could meet up for a drink later.
a No, unfortunately I have a few meetings in the city and then I'm going directly back to Hamburg. **Go to 9.**
b No, sorry, I'm leaving this afternoon. By the way, are you still based in Cape Town? **Go to 2.**

Tom: Thanks, Sam, that's nice to hear. I'm going to wait and see what happens. It might even lead to a job with more responsibility. No reason to move on just yet.
a I understand. Well, here's my card so you know how to reach me if you change your mind. **Go to 9.**
b I understand. Good luck. **Go to 9.**

Tom: Oh, look at the time! I should really run. It was great seeing you again, Sam.
Sam: It was great seeing you too, Tom. Take care.

9 Arne and his assistant manager, Erika, are preparing for a meeting with the web
designer of TopOffice's new website. Listen to the conversation and complete
the collocations.

1 face-to-face . . . .

2 . . . . breakdown

3 sources of possible . . . .

4 . . . . study

5 mutual . . . .

6 to . . . . (someone's) sensitivity to/toward

7 . . . . milestones

8 on an . . . . basis

Now listen to the conversation again. Are the statements true (t) or false (f)?

1   Erika, Arne and the web designer have met before.

2   In the past, a communication problem occurred between the two
companies.

3   Arne believes that people in different fields should always be able to
communicate using email.

4   Arne isn't interested in establishing a long-term relationship with
Fresh_Image.

10 Your firm has hired a new employee from Colombia. Your boss has
asked you to send him an email that welcomes him to your department.   *over to you*
The email should also explain three important aspects of doing business in
Germany: using formal titles (Dr, Mr and Ms) with colleagues, although your
company language is English; being on time; and meeting with business
partners outside of the office. You haven't met the new employee yet, so use
formal language to write the email.

. . . .

. . . .

. . . .

. . . .

. . . .

1 Mary and Frank work together. Match the different ways of talking (a–d) about the future to Frank's responses (1–6). Then underline the future verbs that Frank uses.

a a prediction **c** a firm intention or goal
b a spontaneous offer or promise **d** a prior arrangement or appointment

1 Mary: Have you scheduled a meeting with Fischer Inc.?
Frank: Yes, we're going to meet on Monday at 10 am.

2 Mary: Have you looked at the sales figures from the first quarter?
Frank: Yes. It looks like we'll be able to reach our sales goal by the beginning of the fourth quarter, far ahead of schedule.

3 Mary: I just don't have time to phone the new client today.
Frank: No problem. I'll do it first thing after lunch.

4 Mary: Our help desk staff constantly work 12-hour shifts. We really need to do something.
Frank: I know. We're going to recruit five additional employees by the end of the second quarter.

5 Mary: How do you think Fischer Inc. will react to our offer?
Frank: I think they'll accept it. The offer meets all of their requirements, and I think we're offering a lower price than our competitors.

6 Mary: Happy birthday, Frank! Do you have any big plans for the year?
Frank: Thanks, Mary. Yes, actually, I'm going to quit smoking and travel to Indonesia.

2 **Complete the email using the verbs in brackets and *will*, *to be* + *going to* or the present continuous. Sometimes more than one answer is possible. Explain the reasons for your answers.**

An invitation to tender

Von:	Karolin Herrmann
An:	Richard Forrest Ulrike Kaupert
Cc:	
Betreff:	An invitation to tender
Anlagen:	Agenda_20May.doc, InvTender.doc

| | Agenda_20May.doc | 99 KB |
| | InvTender.doc | 18 KB |

Dear All

José just sent me a very interesting invitation to tender he got this morning. It's attached.

Richard, I know that you're usually responsible for these offers, but since you have other priorities right now I . . . . .¹ (prepare) it myself.

We don't have a lot of time, so I . . . . .² (need) your help:

I . . . . .³ (meet) with the company's project manager next Tuesday.

Richard - could you please calculate the costs for both labour and materials? Could you send this information by Wednesday?

Ulrike - could you please look at our project schedule to see by when we can realistically finish each phase of the job? Could you let me know by Thursday morning?

I . . . . .⁴ (send) you an update next Tuesday after the meeting. As you can see from the attached agenda, we . . . . .⁵ (talk) about this opportunity at our weekly team meeting, so please bring along whatever you've done. Speaking of the meeting, please remember that we . . . . .⁶ (meet) in the third floor conference room this week instead of in my office.

Thanks in advance.

Best
Karolin

3 Who might say what during a conference call? Some phrases might have more than one answer.

a conference call chair
b conference call participant

1 ___ I'm afraid that topic is a bit beyond the scope of today's agenda.

2 ___ I think that more or less covers everything for today.

3 ___ Thank you for participating.

4 ___ Sorry, I didn't quite catch that.

5 ___ Do you mean ...?

6 ___ Can you slow down, please?

7 ___ We're not following you.

8 ___ John sends his apologies. He can't be with us today.

9 ___ I'd just like to check that everybody is connected.

10 ___ Could I just come in here?

11 ___ So, I guess we can get started.

12 ___ Shall we move to the next point on the agenda?

4 Listen to the conference call. Mark the statements as true (t), false (f) or not enough information (n). Correct the false statements.

1 ___ The first point on the agenda is the technical problems that could arise.

2 ___ One technical aspect for the training is the invoicing system.

3 ___ The training in Italy was five days long.

4 ___ In Italy, all help desk staff members participated in the training.

5 ___ Vitale was satisfied with the training.

Listen again and complete the phrases the conference call participants use for interrupting.

1 Sorry, Vitale, I . . . . that. What was the third aspect?

2 Could I . . . .? Do we have a budget for the training?

3 . . . ., but I have a question for Vitale: were all staff members fully trained . . .?

4 Sorry Jan, I was . . . . that the number of staff who are trained and whether . . .

5 If I . . . . for a minute, Jürgen? I think that rather than continuing our conversation . . .

5 Listen to the voicemail message.
🔊 8 Correct Rachel's notes.

Optimization project status
- 14 offers have been
  received and evaluated
- vendors have been
  selected
- orders haven't been
  placed, will be done on
  Tuesday
- timeline has been set,
  Glen has sent it in an
  email

6 Unscramble the questions.

1 A: arrangements / have / travel / the / you / made / already / ?

   . . . .

   B: No, I'm afraid I haven't. I'll get to it this afternoon.

2 A: yet / to / we / invitation / have / the / tender / received / ?

   . . . .

   B: Yes, it arrived a few minutes ago.

3 A: It's nearly 2 pm. lunch / had / have / yet / you / ?

   . . . .

   B: Oh yes, I ate around noon.

4 A: already / from / have / gotten / client / feedback / we / the / ?

   . . . .

   B: No, unfortunately nothing yet.

7 Think of a project you're working on. Write a short email to your
project team leader or supervisor to update him or her on your
progress. Use the present perfect passive in combination with the words
already and *yet*.

over to you

. . . .

. . . .

. . . .

. . . .

. . . .

8 Listen to the questions and answers. Who gives the better answer to each question, Stephanie or Ryan? Why? Whom would you hire?

1 ....

2 ....

3 ....

4 ....

5 ....

6 ....

9 Listen to the audio in exercise 8 again and match the words in the boxes to form collocations you hear. Then use the collocations to complete the sentences.

1	ambitious		a		record
2	best		b		experience
3	interesting		c		goal
4	relevant		d		member
5	team		e		question
6	track		f		candidate

1 I have five years of ....

2 I hope that you'll hire me because I'm the .... for the job.

3 My .... in winning customers speaks for itself.

4 That's an ....

5 I know it sounds like an ....

6 I'd also be satisfied working as a ....

10 Write definitions for the following words. Which term is rather informal?

1 to unwind ....

2 to contribute to ....

3 to be well suited for ....

4 to freak out ....

5 to be distressed ....

6 to overcome ....

11 In a business setting, the word *benefit* can have multiple meanings. Match each sentence or set of sentences to the definition of benefit that is being expressed. If necessary, use a dictionary to help you.

1 Did you go to last year's benefit for the hospital? It brought in over one million Euros for the new treatment centre!

2 One benefit of the training course was being able to talk with people from outside of my department.

3 The job has a great benefits package that includes 20 holiday days per year.

4 Before we decide to move the office, we have to weigh the costs and benefits.

5 I'm afraid I can't buy anything right now, not even food. I haven't gotten this month's unemployment benefit yet.

6 It's true that he doesn't have experience in that area, but he thinks he can do it. I'd like to give him the benefit of the doubt.

a ____ an advantage or profit

b ____ what employees receive from a company in addition to their wages; also called perks

c ____ money or other help that people receive from the government; social welfare help

d ____ to accept something as correct, even if there is information that speaks against it

e ____ an event to collect money to help an organization or person

f ____ to compare the potential losses with the potential gains

12 Use the words in the box to form collocations, phrases or sentences that explain the benefits of team-building activities. Change the word forms as needed.

pay attention • communicate • listen • hear • improve • brainstorm • work together • ideas • solutions • roles • projects • office • outside

1 We can improve our communication with each other by completing ...
tasks that are different from the ones we do in the office ....

2 ....

3 ....

4 ....

5 ....

6 ....

Progress check 1 → page 65

Problem-solving

4

1 Find the words or collocations in the text on page 48 of the coursebook that are synonyms of the definitions.

Unit checklist
- make oral and written summaries
- practise the language of meetings
- write minutes
- discuss tips for effective meetings

1 to change something again

. . . .

2 to be prepared and available to handle something

. . . .

3 to fail to work properly . . . .

4 an on-site appointment . . . .

5 a general review to make sure nothing will go wrong . . . .

6 a technical specialist . . . .

7 not on-site; distant . . . .

8 complete and correct tips . . . .

2 Identify the cause and effect. Then write sentences using the words in brackets. It might be necessary to add information or write two sentences.

1 a mistake by the machine operator / expensive repair bill (led to)

. . . .

2 the meeting started late / the client got lost in the city (so)

. . . .

3 an increase in stock prices / successful launch of a top-selling product
(as a result of this)

. . . .

4 an increase in gasoline prices / an increase in delivery costs (has caused)

. . . .

5 a storm over the Atlantic / a three-hour flight delay (meant)

. . . .

6 the conference call was postponed / technical problems (due to)

. . . .

3 Choose the correct words in each sentence.

1 As/After she was calling her colleague, the train arrived/had arrived.
2 Right before/while he met with the client, he was checking/had checked the dates of the recent on-site repairs.
3 Peter recommended/was recommending a complete support package after/while he had analysed the problems.
4 I got/had gotten the job offer while/after I was attending the trade fair.

Read the sentences again. Which signal words are used with the past continuous and which are used with the past perfect?

Past continuous	Past perfect

4 Complete the email using the verbs in brackets in the correct tenses: past continuous, simple past, present perfect or past perfect.

From: Francesca Robine
To: Sonja Marshall
Cc:
Subject: Bad day!

Hi Sonja

Today has been one terrible day!! First I missed my train. Then as I . . . .[1] (check) my emails this morning, my computer . . . .[2] (stop) working. Guess what? The hard drive had malfunctioned!

Glen, our department's IT specialist, ...[3] (say) that my computer . . . .[4] (not send) any information to the back-up system earlier this week. He said he doesn't know why.

Before the computer . . . .[5] (fail), I . . . .[6] (made) changes to the annual report. Now the entire report is completely gone. I . . . .[7] (save) a copy to a USB stick yesterday, but unfortunately I . . . .[8] (delete) that copy this morning.

And then, while I . . . .[9] (talk) to Glen about the computer, my telephone . . . .[10] (ring). It was my new boss, Kara, calling to check on the status of the report.

I know that last week I . . . .[11] (promise) I'd go to lunch with you today, but so far my day . . . .[12] (be) a disaster! Can we reschedule for next week?

Franzi

5 Listen to the audio. Are the statements true (t) or false (f)?

10

1   Ms Müller's company matches employees with companies.

2   Ms Smith-Böhm dislikes working early in the day.

3   The company has mostly German employees.

4   The company buys plastic components for cars.

5   The company might need a new manager.

6   Ms Smith-Böhm would like to have a permanent job.

Listen again and write the two phrases used by Ms Smith-Böhm to summarize the information.

1 ....

2 ....

6 You are Ms Müller. Write an email to Ms Smith-Böhm that summarizes your conversation.

over to you

....

....

....

....

....

7 Listen to the conference call. Complete the table with the phrases that each person uses to agree or disagree with the ideas related to each agenda item.

11

	Teamwork	Recent orders
Bill	1	4
Patricia	2	5
Harshad	3	6

Put the number for each phrase on the spectrum to indicate the degree of disagreement or agreement.

Strongly disagree	Neutral opinion	Strongly agree

8 Change the sentences from active to passive as needed in order to make Patricia's email to her staff less direct.

From:	Patricia Ross
To:	✉ Susanna Marks, Leonard Stark, Rachele Kuhn
Cc:	
Subject:	Customer survey follow up

Dear All

I've received the results from a recent customer service survey. The results were not particularly positive. In sum, we aren't being hired by the clients for additional services. We need to reevaluate our strategy. We can't expect the clients to contact us. . . . .
. . . . .¹

I suggest the following:
Our sales team must contact the clients immediately after the service is carried out.
. . . . .²

We should improve our databases to better track this information.
. . . . .³

You need to update me about our progress on a weekly basis.
. . . . .⁴

Let's meet next Friday morning at 10 am to talk about this and delegate tasks.

Best
Patti

9 Rewrite the notes from a board meeting using the passive.

Research results:
- We have a market share of 5 per cent in the Middle East (1)
- All our current staff overworked, satisfaction low (2)

Board decisions:
- Increase staff by 10 per cent
  -> Deadline: May next year (3)
- Distribute profits to shareholders
  -> Deadline: third quarter (4)

At the next meeting:
- Finance Committee to present current status of investments (5)
- Mergers & acquisitions department update by Mr Lopez (6)

Tip Avoid using *we* and *our* in formal minutes: use *the company* instead. Always use *by* when expressing a deadline.

1 (find) It was found that the company's market share is ....
...5 per cent in the Middle East. ....

2 (show) ....

3 (decide) ....

4 (decide) ....

5 (present) ....

6 (give) ....

Did you know?

In general, BE more frequently uses *has been decided* (present perfect passive) and AE more frequently uses *was decided* (simple past passive), but both phrases have the same meaning.

10 Complete the crossword puzzle using vocabulary from pp. 54–55.

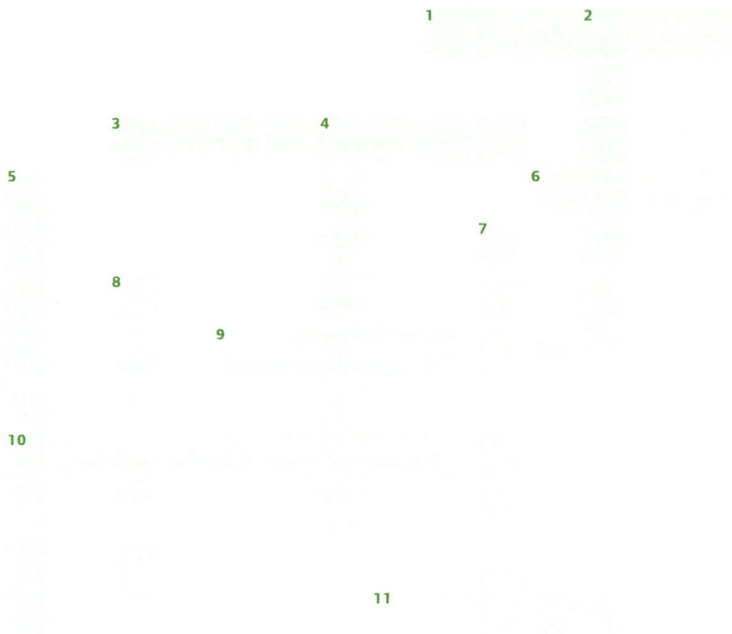

Across

1 (v) to share, tell

3 (adj) not taking one side of a matter; not letting a personal opinion affect one's decision or perspective

6 (v) to connect with someone

9 (adj) communicated fully in as few words as possible

10 (adj) able to produce something or reach a result

11 (n) a feeling of dislike toward a person due to something negative that happened in the past

Down

2 (v) to give someone a role connected to carrying out specific tasks

4 (v) to distribute or assign

5 (n) information accepted as fact without confirmation

7 (n) an agreement by a group

8 (n) an abbreviation that uses the first letters of each word in the full title

1 Think about the last presentation you gave. Analyse your audience using complete sentences. After you've analysed your audience, think about the presentation you gave. If you gave the same presentation tomorrow, would you change anything? Why or why not?

Role in the company/organization . . . .

Reason for attending the presentation . . . .

Experience with/knowledge of the topic . . . .

Technical background/education . . . .

Age . . . . Gender . . . .

Nationality . . . .

2 Listen to the conversation and complete the sentences.

🎧 12

1 We . . . . you a bonus if you . . . . the new position in two weeks instead of the usual four or eight weeks.

2 If we . . . ., our reputation . . . .

3 If the client . . . . with our work, they . . . . very clear that they worked with us in the past.

4 If you . . . . instead of the usual four, we . . . . in addition to your first year's salary.

5 If I . . . . your offer to begin in two weeks, ... about offering me the job?

3 Complete the sentences with the correct form of the conditional (first or second).

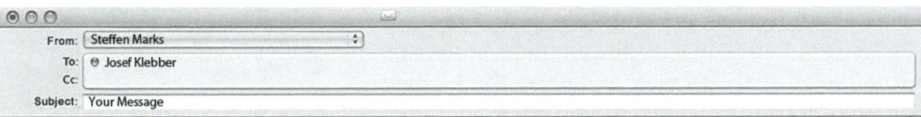

Hi Josef

I just got your message. Since I only have a few minutes between all my meetings and appointments today, I thought I'd write you a quick email.

It sounds like you really have a dilemma. I don't like that they might take back the job offer if you decide not to start in two weeks.

Here are a few things to think about:

- Would it help if you . . . . .¹ (not start) in two weeks but in three?
- If you said that you wanted a 30% bonus instead of 20%, and they agreed to that,

  .² (will) that 10% change your decision?

- If you left your current position in two weeks instead of four, ...³ (will) you worry about your reputation at your current company?

- If you .⁴ (talk) to your boss at your current company, would he understand or would it ruin your relationship with him?

Even though I've listed all these questions, honestly, if I . . . . .⁵ (be) you,

I .⁶ (accept) the new job. It's a great opportunity. You know you can't

advance any further in your current company and position. If you . . . . .⁷

(be) older, I .⁸ (say) stay where you are. But that's not the situation.

When you leave your current company for this job offer or for any other, I know it . . . .

. . . . .⁹ (be) difficult for you. It's a great company and you have fantastic coworkers. But you need to be challenged in your job, too!

I've got to run to my next meeting. I hope this helps. In case you .¹⁰

(want) to call me tomorrow, I'll be in my office after 11.

Good luck!

Best
Steffen

4 Listen to the dialogue in exercise 2 and read the email in exercise 3
again. If you were Josef, what would you do and why? Would you
follow any of Steffen's advice? (Tip: Use the second conditional.)

over to you

. . . .

. . . .

. . . .

. . . .

. . . .

5 Complete the sentences in the dialogue using the third conditional.

Steffen: So, what happened when you met with the personnel manager?

Josef: Well, I told her that it was a very difficult decision, but that according to my contract with my current company I had to give at least four weeks' notice. She said that she understood, but that she had spoken with the other candidate and that even though he wasn't their top choice, he was willing to start in two weeks instead of four.

Steffen: Wow. That's too bad. So they took back the entire offer.

Josef: That's right.

Steffen: If you . . . .[1] (know) that, ...

. . . .[2] (you change) your answer?

Josef: I don't know. I don't think so.

Steffen: Did you know that they had also offered the job to the other top candidate?

Josef: No, I didn't.

Steffen: They didn't tell you they were going to do that?

Josef: If they . . . .[3] (tell) me, I think I . . . .

. . . .[4] (think) about the offer more carefully.

Steffen: But if you . . . .[5] (know) that, ...

. . . .[6] (it change) your decision? Honestly?

Josef: No, I don't think so. I need to respect my current contract. My current employer has really been great, you know.

Steffen: I can understand that. But it's too bad your position isn't more challenging.

Josef: Right. Look, here come our lunches. Perfect timing.

Steffen: Wow. If I . . . .[7] (know) the pasta would

look so delicious, I . . . .[8] (order) it too!

6 Read the sentences from an introduction to a presentation. Then put them in the correct order (1–8).

a [ ] My talk will last about 15 minutes, and I'd be happy to take your questions after the presentation.

b [ ] On average, Worthington International has helped companies improve their financial performance by between 5 and 7 per cent.

c [ ] Good morning, ladies and gentlemen.

d [ ] So let's start with my first point, our bookkeeping and payroll services.

e [ ] Thank you for inviting me here today to talk about the financial services we're able to offer your company.

f [ ] Today I'm going to discuss three main points. First of all, I'll tell you about our bookkeeping and payroll services; then I'll move on to our auditing services; and finally, I'll tell you a little bit about our investment management services.

g [ ] As members of the finance committee, I'm sure you're interested in learning how we can help your company do the same!

h [ ] My name is Enrico Rodriguez, and I'm the client relations manager at Worthington International.

🎧 13 Listen to check your answers.

7 Effective hooks are often interesting facts, rhetorical questions (a question you don't expect people to answer but rather think about) or stories or anecdotes (a true short story that is entertaining or interesting). For each topic, write what you could use as an interesting fact, a rhetorical question or a story or anecdote to help open the presentation.

1 India as an emerging market

Fact: Not only does India have the second-largest population in the world; with nearly 1/3 of its population under the age of 15, its population is also very young.

Rhetorical question: Is now the time to enter the Indian market?

Anecdote: When I was in Mumbai in 2010 attending an international conference, I had the opportunity to speak with ...

2 Your company as a competent partner

. . . .

. . . .

. . . .

. . . .

3 Your country as a tourist destination

. . . .

. . . .

. . . .

. . . .

4 Your city or town as an ideal business location

. . . .

. . . .

. . . .

. . . .

8 **Listen to the endings of four presentations. For each, write a summary**
14 **sentence that includes the audience's objectives and benefits. Several answers**
are possible.

1 If you're productive during the year and complete the necessary . . .

steps, you'll get a bonus. . . . .

By being productive during the year and completing the necessary . .

steps, you'll get a bonus. . . . .

2 In other words, if you . . . .

. . . .

3 So, by . . . ., you . . . .

. . . .

4 In sum, if you . . . .

. . . .

. . . .

Tip *economic* (adj.) means something has
to do with economics
economical (adj.) means a good value

9 Match the words in the boxes to form collocations. Then use four of the collocations to complete the sentences.

1	emerging	a	network
2	significant	b	relationship
3	entry	c	inventory
4	personalized	d	mode
5	extensive	e	market
6	to track	f	factor

1 Our . . . . of distributors includes Indonesia and Malaysia.

2 We aim to develop a . . . . with each of our clients.

3 The most . . . . in the decision was the vendor's experience in South America.

4 Some experts believe that China will be the most important . . . .

10 Unscramble the words to form sentences that can be used at the end of a presentation.

1 financial services / brief / of / that / our / a / was / overview / .

. . . .

2 main / let / to / me / conclude / the / points / just / review / . / ,

. . . .

3 today / brings / that / to / of / the / me / my / presentation / end / .

. . . .

4 wraps / just / that / about / up / things / .

. . . .

5 idea / that's / you / I / services / hope / given / our / of / some / .

. . . .

11 Complete the noun/verb word pairs.

1 . . . . / to acknowledge
2 commitment / . . . .
3 congratulations / . . . .
4 gratification / . . . .
5 identity / . . . .

6 . . . . / to imagine
7 . . . . / to tempt
8 . . . . / to trick
9 . . . . / to satisfy

1 Which type of visual would be best for presenting each set of information? Match the types of visuals (a–f) to the sets of information (1–4) There are two answers you don't need.

a	bar chart	**d**	pie chart
b	flow chart	**e**	table
c	line graph	**f**	timeline

1 You are preparing a presentation for your company's shareholders and want to show how revenue has developed at your company between 2008 and this year.

2 Your company sells five different products. You are giving a presentation to all employees and want to show the percentage of sales of each product type sold last year.

3 You are giving a presentation to new employees and need to show the development of the company starting from its founding in 1972.

4 You are giving a presentation to your department and want to illustrate the amount of revenue received for four different products during the second quarter.

For the two answers that remain, give an example of the kind of information they could illustrate.

2 Listen to two descriptions of the visual. Compare and contrast the descriptions. Which is more effective for the audience?

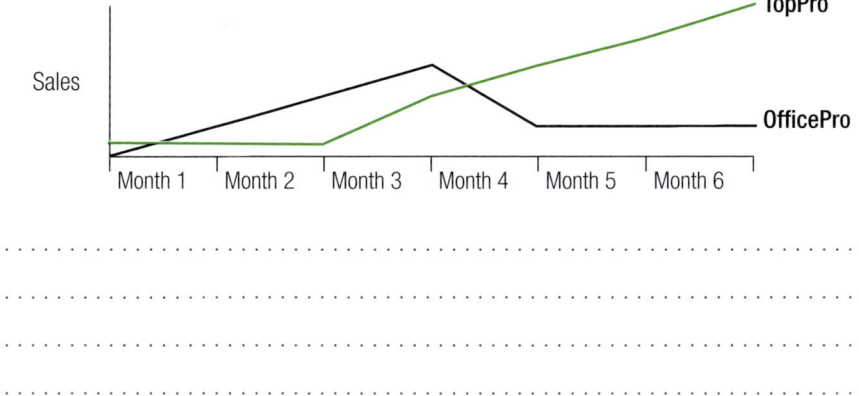

. . . .

. . . .

. . . .

. . . .

3 Write sentences using the information in the table. Use comparative and superlative forms. Several answers are possible.

	Germany	Ireland	Mongolia	Vietnam
Population	82.3 million	4.47 million	2.76 million	87.8 million
GDP per capita	36,332 USD	39,562 USD	1,503 USD	835 USD
Unemployment rate	7.7%	11.9%	3.6%	2.4 %

Did you know?

"GDP per capita" means Gross Domestic Product per person. A country's GDP is the total value of what is produced (goods or products) or provided (services) over one year. To calculate the amount per capita, the GDP is divided by the number of people living in the country.

Sources: OECD "Society at a Glance: Asia/Pacific 2011" (information for 2009); OECD Statistical Profile of Germany (information for 2009); OECD Statistical Profile of Ireland (information for 2009); United Nations Department of Economic and Social Affairs: Population Division, Population Estimates and Projections Section.

1 Population: Germany, Mongolia and Vietnam

. . . .

. . . .

2 GDP per capita: Vietnam and Mongolia

. . . .

. . . .

3 GDP per capita: Germany and Ireland

. . . .

. . . .

4 Unemployment rate: Germany and Ireland

. . . .

. . . .

4 Match the linking words (1–7) with their functions (a–f). One function must be used twice.

1	nonetheless	**a**		to present a result
2	similarly	**b**		to present additional information that is similar to the previous information
3	consequently			
4	moreover	**c**		to present a contrast
5	namely	**d**		to present a specific example or details
6	therefore	**e**		to show how a subject or idea is the same as or has something in common with the previous subject or idea
7	whereas			
		f		to present information that is not expected to follow the previous idea

5 Add the linking words and transitions in the box to the text from the middle of a presentation. It might be necessary to adjust some sentences. Use the explanations in exercise 4 to help you.

> now let's turn to • consequently • moreover •
> moving on • nonetheless • therefore • whereas

_∨ Moving on, let's

~~Let's~~ look at Namibia. Our sales have been steadily increasing in Namibia since entering the market there three years ago. Our competitors have decided to leave the country entirely. We have chosen to increase our sales efforts there. Since our competitors are leaving, I know it might appear as if our success will be easy. We need to continue our focused marketing efforts and launch products specifically tailored to customers in the country. Today I'd like to propose adapting three of our top-selling products in South Africa for the Namibian market. I'd also like to propose reviewing the products that are already selling very well in Namibia to ensure that they are meeting the needs of the buyers 100 per cent. We'll need to develop product assessment methods specific to the Namibian market. Well, those are our rather ambitious plans for Namibia. Our next topic is our rather poor performance in Kenya.

6 The phrase *used to* can be utilized to talk about the present or past. Which sentences refer to the present and which sentences refer to the past?

a present
b past

1   He isn't used to travelling for work. He only goes on one business trip a year.

2   Did he use to be based in Singapore?

3   My supervisor didn't use to hold weekly department meetings. Now it's a priority.

4   The supplier used to deliver the pipes promptly. However, during the last six months every delivery has been late

5   The company's CEO is used to being in the news. The company she founded has transformed the computer industry.

6   Is the new colleague used to answering financial questions? If not, we should make sure another person from the department is there to help him at the end of the presentation.

Complete the rules by adding *did, infinitive verb, to be* or *verb+ing*.

When used for the present: (subject) . . . . used to + ...

for questions: . . . . + (subject) used to + ...

When used for the past: (subject) used to + ...

for questions: . . . . + (subject) use to + ...

7 Form sentences or questions. Add words or change word forms as needed.

1 Jenny / used to / attend / the trade fairs / ?

. . . .

2 OfficePro / not used to / be / the top-selling product / .

. . . .

3 Ravi / used to / work / for your company / ?

. . . .

4 Jose / be used to / make / field visits / ?

. . . .

5 Our competitors / be used to / have / low sales in Namibia / .

. . . .

6 Matthew / be not used to / live / in a country with such cold weather / .

. . . .

8 **Complete the responses to questions during a presentation using the sentences in the box. Some responses could have more than one answer.**

> Oh, that's a good question. • I see what you mean. • Can we come back to that later? • Sorry, I don't know the answer to that, but I will find out.

1 . . . . I'm fairly certain the information I'll present in a few minutes will answer your question.

2 . . . . Could you please see me immediately after the presentation so I can get your contact information? I'd be happy to send you the answer within the next week.

3 . . . . That's a point I don't address in my presentation today, but we'll definitely need to consider it for our next meeting in six weeks.

4 . . . . Well, we thought that our efforts to increase production would also increase our efficiency. Unfortunately, that's not what happened.

5 . . . . If I understand you correctly, you'd like to know why we've chosen to outsource our help desk. Well, we looked at different options and …

6 . . . . I'd like to say more about that when we discuss last year's expenses.

🔊16 **Listen to check your answers.**

9 Read the definitions and unscramble the words to form collocations found in the report on pages 80–81 of the coursebook.

Definitions		Words	
1	private, secret information	tdnnfoealcii taad	. . . .
2	where people can reclaim misplaced property	tols nda fudno	. . . .
3	companies or people hired by an airport to carry out tasks, such as construction	airport rnocttaocsr	. . . .
4	each flight is assigned to one of these locations; from here people generally exit the airport building directly onto their planes	tpueadrrer ateg	. . . .
5	a place at an airport where all passengers are monitored	rysucite khnietocpc	. . . .
6	where people can buy books, food or other products	tielar bshsetltneaim	. . . .
7	regular airport employees	airport nlnpeores	. . . .
8	errors that are unintelligent	pdsiut kiaetsms	. . . .
9	a plan one has in his or her mind	nlaemt gyrsteta	. . . .
10	steps you take to make sure your property is safe	yresitcu emaersus	. . . .

10 Choose one graphic from page 80 in the coursebook and describe it as you would present it in a presentation. Use the Tip box on page 36 of this Workbook unit to help you structure your description.

over to you

At CDG Paris, fewer laptops are lost each week than at AMS Amsterdam.

More misplaced laptops are reclaimed before flights in the US than in

Europe. . . . .

. . . .

. . . .

. . . .

. . . .

☑ Progress check 2 → page 67

1 Complete the sentences with the words in the box.

suppose • be open • be interested • may not • can't consider • be better

Unit checklist
- report what people have said
- practise the language of negotiations
- use tentative language
- discuss negotiation strategies

1 Well, I . . . . things may change.

2 Mightn't it . . . . to talk about the details later?

3 And what would you . . . . in at the moment?

4 I'm afraid we . . . . such a large quantity at the moment.

5 Might you also . . . . to a slightly different proposal?

6 We . . . . be able to consider the proposal as it stands.

2 Use four of the sentences from exercise 1 to complete the dialogue.

Richard: I know that it's an excellent offer, but I'm terribly sorry, it simply isn't possible.

Oksana: . . . . [1]

Richard: Ideally we'd like 20,000 units at 1.35 Euro each.

Oksana: I see. . . . . [2] What about 30,000 units at 1.30 each?

Richard: Your offer of 1.30 per unit is appealing, but . . . . [3] It's simply too high. I've been given strict orders – the quantity is non-negotiable – we can't go above 20,000 right now.

Oksana: . . . . [4]

🎧 17 **Listen to check your answers.**

3 Read the examples and complete the rules. Then rewrite the simple present and present continuous statements and question using reported speech.

> The negotiations **are** this morning.

He said that the negotiations <u>were</u> this morning.

She told me that the negotiations <u>were taking place</u> in Conference Room C.

> The negotiations **are taking place** in Conference Room C.

> **Is** Maria in the office on Tuesdays?

He wanted to know if/whether Maria <u>was</u> in the office on Tuesdays.

Rules for the simple present and present continuous in reported speech

In reported speech, simple present statements and questions change to

. . . . verb forms.

In reported speech, present continuous statements and questions change to

. . . . verb forms.

In reported speech, the reporting verb . . . . requires an object.

When forming questions in reported speech, it is necessary to use the words

. . . . or . . . . to introduce the restated question

and change the word order.

1 "The team leader is extremely competent."

He said . . . .

2 "No, the legal department isn't reviewing the contract."

She told . . . .

3 "Does he go to the committee meetings?"

She wanted to know . . . .

> **Tip** If questions in direct speech do not contain a question word, use *if* or *whether* in reported speech. If questions in direct speech contain a question word such as *how many, what, where, when*, use the question word in reported speech.

4 Read the examples and complete the rules. Then rewrite the simple past, present perfect, past continuous, present perfect continuous and past perfect statements and questions using reported speech.

> The customer **expected** an immediate response.

He said that the customer <u>had expected</u> an immediate response.

She warned me that they <u>hadn't met</u> the project milestones on time.

> We **haven't met** the project milestones on time.

> We**'ve been waiting** for the answer.

She mentioned that they <u>had been waiting</u> for the answer.

At the press conference, he revealed that the company <u>had known</u> about the problem for three weeks.

> The company **had known** about the problem for three weeks.

Rules for the simple past, present perfect, past continuous, present perfect continuous and past perfect in reported speech

In reported speech, the simple past and present perfect change to

. . . . and past continuous and present perfect continuous

change to . . . . verb forms.

In reported speech, past perfect statements/questions do / do not change form.

The reporting verb . . . . requires an object.

1 "They wanted to talk with you about the late delivery."

He warned . . . .

2 "I haven't checked my email all day."

She said . . . .

3 "Have they been working on the strategic plan?"

He wondered . . . .

4 "Before it rose in 2009, it had plummeted to $10.36 per share."

They noted . . . .

5 Read the examples and complete the rules. Then rewrite the sentences with modals using reported speech.

> Fred **will be tired** when he arrives.

She said that Fred <u>would be tired</u> when he arrived.

> Michele **can organize** a short tour for him.

He pointed out that Michele <u>could organize</u> a short tour for him.

> We **may want** to schedule the meeting for after lunch.

She suggested that we <u>might want</u> to schedule the meeting for after lunch.

> When **could** he **take** the train?

She asked when he <u>could take</u> the train.

> It **might be** too late to book a flight.

He pointed out that it <u>might be</u> too late to book a flight.

> It **would be** a good idea to call the hotel to confirm the reservation.

She said it <u>would be</u> a good idea to call the hotel to confirm the reservation.

> The train **should arrive** on time.

He noted that the train <u>should arrive</u> on time.

Rules for modals in reported speech

In reported speech, the verbs *will*, *can* and *may* do / do not change form.
In reported speech, the verbs *could*, *might*, *would* and *should* do / do not change form.

1 "Won't you see him at the trade fair in August?"

   She asked . . . .

2 "We can forget about catching our flight."

   He said . . . .

3 "Why wouldn't you export to Mongolia? Consumption is soaring at the moment."

   He wondered . . . .

4 "The task force should set clear priorities."

   She pointed out . . . .

6 **Read the examples and complete the rules. Then rewrite the sentences using reported speech.**

Our boss says that the negotiations with this company <u>are</u> always difficult.

> The negotiations with this company **are** always difficult.

> The negotiations **have been** difficult this year.

She says that the negotiations <u>have been</u> difficult this year.

They say we <u>won't be able</u> to work with them again.

> We **won't be able** to work with them again.

Rules for reporting verbs in the simple present

Reporting verbs can be in the simple present.

If the reporting verb is in the simple present, the verb in the reported speech does / does not change form.

1 "Our workshops promote teamwork."

They say . . . .

2 "The incentives aren't enough to motivate employees."

The committee insists . . . .

3 "We weren't able to convince them to accept the offer."

She says . . . .

Did you know?

In English, it's not possible to use a special verb form to express doubt when reporting what a person said. In written English, doubt can only be expressed by adding an additional statement that specifically expresses doubt. However, when speaking, one can express doubt in what a person said by emphasizing or stressing the reporting verb. If necessary, an additional statement that expresses doubt is added.
Written English: She said she would finish the report by Tuesday, but in my opinion it's doubtful.
Spoken English: She *said* she would finish the report by Tuesday (but you never know).

---

7 **Match the sentence halves.**

1	I hope he doesn't bring	**a**	up with an offer that we can't refuse.
2	I'd like to point	**b**	away, but we seem to have reached a deadlock.
3	I'm not worried. They've always managed to come	**c**	out that we have been a reliable supplier for the past 10 years.
4	We don't want to walk	**d**	down every idea we've brought to the table.
5	Let me put	**e**	up another irrelevant point after the break.
6	We'd like to compromise, but so far you've turned	**f**	forward another idea.

8 Using some of the phrasal verbs in exercise 7, describe what happened during the last negotiation you attended. As an alternative, describe what happened during the role-play from exercise 8 on page 93 in the coursebook. Remember to use the correct forms of reported speech.

over to you

. . . .

. . . .

. . . .

9 Listen to the audio and answer the questions. Then read the transcript and
18 underline the tentative language used.

1 How many electric-powered cars does Simon want to buy?
2 What are the reasons Simon's company wants to add electric-powered cars to its corporate fleet?
3 What is Roger's initial offer?
4 What is Simon's desired price?
5 What concession does Roger ask Simon to make?
6 What reason does Roger give for not selling the electric-powered cars for 19,000 Euro each?
7 What is the final agreement?

10 Find verb + noun collocations in the text on pages 94–95 of the coursebook that match the definitions.

1 to create a relationship that is key to achieving your company's goals

. . . .

2 to keep the connections with your business partners positive

. . . .

3 to establish limits

. . . .

4 to allow someone to have some flexibility

. . . .

5 to lose willingness to wait

. . . .

6 to be aware of the different parts involved

. . . .

1 **Complete the online reviews with the words in the boxes.**

annoying · confused · furious · frustrated

Save your money – don't come here! First our waiter became . . . .[1] when we couldn't read the menu. He didn't offer us an international menu, so maybe they didn't have one. When we became . . . .[2] by the bill and the money as we were trying to pay (it was our first day in the country), the waiter got absolutely . . . .[3] and almost started yelling at us. In addition, the music that was playing in the restaurant, some sort of local folk music, was extremely loud and . . . .[4]. I think there were only two different songs during our entire dinner!

embarrassing · irritated · puzzled · surprised

When we checked into the B&B, we noticed that our host was unhappy with us – or . . . .[5] with us – for some reason. At first we couldn't figure out what was wrong – and he didn't say anything to us – but then we realized that we probably forgot to mention that our dog, Mimi, is a dog and not a child! We think he was probably . . . .[6] and . . . .[7]. For this reason, the process of checking in was a little . . . .[8] for us. Overall, though, we had a great time.

delighted · enthusiastic · fascinating · stunning

We took our boss here for dinner for his 65th birthday because he loves Middle Eastern food. Now I understand why this restaurant was recommended to me. Our waiters had a lot of energy – they were extremely . . . .[9] about the restaurant and wanted to make sure we had a great night. The belly-dancing show was simply . . . .[10]. The women looked . . . .[11] in their costumes. Our boss was . . . .[12] by the entire evening – he even stopped by our offices the next day to tell us how much he enjoyed it. Highly recommended!

2 Unscramble the sentences or questions that are speculations.

1 today / must / she / teleworking / be / .
A: Has anyone seen Anne?

B: No, sorry. . . . .

2 can't / true / gossip / the / simply / be / office / !
A: Have you heard the news? We're to be taken over by a French company.

B: I can't imagine that. . . . .

3 wondering / be / we've / concessions / she / so many / must / why / offered / .
A: We're sure to close the deal tomorrow. We've given her a lot to think about.

B: Yes. . . . .

4 he / could / joking / be / ?
A: Did you get Mischa's email about the new formal dress code?

B: That seems highly unlikely. . . . .

Wait a minute, isn't today April 1?

5 your / impressed / sales / he / be / by / skills / must / .
A: I've just closed my third contract this week.

B: Have you told Simon? . . . .

6 might / frustrated / they / little / be / a / ?
A: I still haven't gotten an answer from the Indonesian supplier.

B: Well, you haven't offered much of a compromise. . . . .

. . . .

Tip Does this look familiar?
If I had heard about the company's entry into the stock exchange, I could have bought shares.
The construction *modal + have + past participle* is also used in the third conditional. (See pages 64 and 70 of the coursebook.)

3 Complete the sentences about past events using the modals with *have* + past participle or *have been* + *-ing*.

1 A: You know, Robert was looking for you on Monday. He said he needed the latest test results from the lab.

B: Was he? . . . . (he/could/ask) Susanna for them.

A: I don't think he knew she had access to them.

2 A: I'm so frustrated! I put so much time into the RFP and now we don't have a chance of getting the job. We missed the 5 pm deadline because I didn't get a response about the financials from corporate office until 6 pm.

B: . . . . (they/must/meet) with clients all day. Remember the message they sent last week? Representatives from the new key account were in town. Many employees from head office were involved.

3 A: I'm not sure why I haven't been chosen again. Every time Maria asks for volunteers to lead a smaller project, I always say I'm interested – just like in today's meeting. She never chooses me, though.

B: Yeah, I know. But . . . . (she / might not / hear) you. You were sitting in the back corner. The sound doesn't carry very well in that room.

4 A: I'm not sure why I didn't get the job. I have great qualifications and I had two great internships – one was even abroad!

B: . . . . (they/could/look) for someone with more professional experience?

A: . . . . (that/might/be) the problem. The advert did say that candidates should have 2 to 3 years of business experience. I was hoping that the references from my internships would impress them so much they'd be willing to give me a chance.

5 A: You know, Irina didn't invite me on the trip to visit the new factory in Hungary. I really wanted to see the new facilities.

B: . . . . (she/might/wait) for information from you about your availability? You told me that you had to write to her because you had a personal conflict with the proposed dates.

4 Listen to the interview and correct Simone's notes.

🎧 19

Hans Meier

East Coast Manager

Two more offices will be opened this year

Company is in the US market because the company is growing and is still

open to new customers

In business: 16 years

Entered the European market five years ago

Concerns: that plastic won't be around much longer

Equipment recycles plastic

Idea developed in Europe: recycling standards are high

Listen again and write down three open questions and three closed questions that are asked by Simone.

. . . .

. . . .

. . . .

. . . .

. . . .

. . . .

Did you know?

When working with international colleagues to gather information, you might hear someone refer to the "5Ws": *who*, *what*, *where*, *when* and *why*. Along with the word *how*, these words can help you think about what questions you need ask to get the information you need.

5 Draw lines between the words in the three columns to form open and closed questions.

1	How	would it be	a hypothetical situation for a moment?
2	What	do you think	Sam to join the new office?
3	Could	do you plan	the advantage of postponing the negotiation?
4	When	you consider	possible for you to give us a rough estimate?
5	Why	we persuade	to deal with seasonal factors?
6	Shall	would be	we're struggling to reach a consensus?

6 Sort the phrases used for interest-based bargaining in the box into the correct categories.

> How about doing something different? •
> I understand your position. • Perhaps it
> would be a good idea to … • So you're
> saying that … • I'm afraid there's another
> issue … • I'd like to hear your
> perspective. • Can I explain how I see
> things from my perspective? • Can you
> suggest a solution? • I understand your
> concern. • You probably didn't realize
> that …

Asking for your business partner's opinion

. . . .

. . . .

Restating or affirming your partner's position or perspective

. . . .

. . . .

. . . .

Explaining / Offering a suggestion / Voicing an opinion or concern

. . . .

. . . .

. . . .

. . . .

. . . .

7 **Use some phrases from exercise 6 to complete the negotiation.**

Mr Meyer: It seems that we've almost run out of options. You know we'd be happy to do business with you. . . . .[1]

Mr Thomas: Sure. But first I need to give you more background on the business environment we're facing right now. When we sat down this afternoon, ...[2] my company has been trying to deal with incredible financial pressure. Our operation budget has actually decreased from last year.

Mr Meyer: . . . .[3] you won't be making any investments this year?

Mr Thomas: Not exactly. . . . .[4] consider long-term rental agreements – leases – for these machines.

Mr Meyer: . . . .[5] From your perspective, leasing might be your only choice.

Mr Thomas: Yes, that's right. But . . . .[6] It seems that due to the financial crises, many small towns and cities are cutting back their recycling efforts. As a result, we expect the demand for our services – and our current facilities – to decrease within the next 12 months.

Mr Meyer: . . . .[7], and I really appreciate your openness about your current business situation. However, it seems to me that given all these financial pressures you'll have to improve your efficiency just to break even and stay in the market. . . . .[8]. Maybe we could look into a lease-to-own arrangement?

🔊 20 **Listen to check your answers.**

8 **Think of a multinational company in your country. Which characteristics of that company reflect national culture and which its multinational corporate culture?**

over to you

1 Listen to the radio interview. If necessary, correct
🔊21 the statements to make them true.

1 The name of the radio show is Environmental Earthlings.
2 Bernd's company only works with UV disinfection.
3 The key customers include municipalities.
4 In the past, chloride has been used to disinfect water.
5 UV can always be used to disinfect water.

2 Complete the email with the phrases in the box.

> unless anyone has any objections or time conflicts, •
> , replacing Mona Redmond • , so we each need to make an
> extra effort to make sure that we • directly via email or
> phone • as a result, • , ensuring that we stick to the budget
> and meet tight deadlines

Cc:

Subject: Your Message

Dear All

My name is Henk van der Velde, and I've just been appointed as team leader for the water investigation project in Amsterdam . . . .[1]. You've probably heard that Mona has been promoted to a senior management position. My responsibilities are the same as Mona's were: I'll supervise the project . . . .[2].

In regard to internal communications, I am aware that our team is dispersed . . . .[3] always work together. . . . .[4] I hope that each of you takes action and communicates any issue that comes up or that you think might come up. You're always welcome to contact me . . . .[5]. In addition, I'd like to schedule weekly conference calls in order to stay in touch. According to the notes Mona left for me, she held conference calls every Tuesday at 3 pm, Amsterdam time. . . . .[6] I'd like to stick with that schedule.

I'm looking forward to working with you!

Best
Henk

3 Complete the collocations. (If you need help, look at exercise 5 on page 115 of the coursebook.) Then find five phrases in the email in exercise 2 that have similar meanings to four of the collocations.

1 to . . . . collaboratively   5 to . . . . problems

2 to show . . . .   6 to fall through . . . .

3 to . . . . a process   7 to work on a . . . .

4 to . . . . communication

4 Complete the rules.

We'll be handling the customer satisfaction surveys during August. While in China, they'll be establishing new business contacts.

To form the future continuous, use . . . . + verb + ing.

We will have assessed the customer satisfaction surveys by September 1. Unfortunately, the presentation will have ended within the hour.

To form the future perfect, use . . . . + past participle.

A team leader is going on holiday and is checking in with a project team member. Complete the dialogue using the future continuous or future perfect.

A: I'll be back from vacation in three weeks – that's the week of the 21st. What do you think you . . . . .¹ (complete) by then?

B: Realistically? Phase A, if we're lucky. Our project partners just provided the specifications yesterday.

A: I see. So what . . . . .² (you deal) with for the next five to ten days?

B: Well, we . . . . .³ (design) the equipment and . . . . .⁴ (communicate) with the manufacturer during the next week. That should complete Phase A. While we're finishing the design, the manufacturer . . . . .⁵ (procure) the parts they need.

A: When do you expect the design to be completed?

B: I'm hoping that we . . . . .⁶ (complete) the design within two weeks. So that takes us to the 14th. And you're back on the 21st?

A: That's right.

B: By the 21st we . . . .[7] (start) the first step in Phase B, which requires work on site.

A: You . . . .[8] (not finish) the on-site work by the 21st?

B: No, I'm afraid not.

a) **Now underline the phrases that describe a cutoff date or deadline in the future. Which prepositions do you find?**

b) **Circle phrases describing an ongoing period. What are the prepositions or relative adverbs of time?**

5 **Circle the relative pronouns and underline the relative clause. Then identify whether the relative clause in each sentence is defining (d) or non-defining (n).**

1   The client who called yesterday complimented our new service plan.

2   Aweco's CEO, who was at the trade fair in Frankfurt, will be in town next Wednesday.

3   The man whose computer was stolen at the airport is employed by our biggest competitor.

4   The financial report that was issued yesterday included three interesting ideas for increasing our profit margin.

5   Version 2.0 of the technical manual, which was written by Erik, describes the functions in more detail than past versions.

6 **Context plays a role in choosing the correct type of relative clause. Choose the correct sentences.**

1   Before we make recommendations about how your water should be disinfected, we analyze it through a series of tests.

   a   These tests which take less than a week to process and analyze, check for the presence of biological microorganisms as well as man-made chemicals.

   b   These tests, which take less than a week to process and analyze, check for the presence of biological microorganisms as well as man-made chemicals.

2 Rather than simply send you a printout of the results, we believe that it's important to review the findings with you during a face-to-face meeting.

    a   As a result, we employ technicians who are trained environmental specialists and are up-to-date with the most recent quality standards to go over the test results with you in detail.

    b   As a result, we employ technicians, who are trained environmental specialists and are up-to-date with the most recent quality standards, to go over the test results with you in detail.

3 Based on the information discussed with the technician, we create a proposal to improve your water quality. There's no limit to the quantity of water that can be cleaned.

    a   We provide solutions for municipalities which serve only 200 people up through to major towns and cities serving millions of people.

    b   We provide solutions for municipalities, which serve only 200 people, up through to major towns and cities serving millions of people.

7 **Relative clauses can be used to combine ideas so that short, uninteresting sentences can be avoided. Edit the paragraph from an external report by adding relative clauses to and combining sentences in the highlighted text.**

> **Did you know?**
>
> In a defining relative clause that describes objects or situations, British English uses *which* and American English uses *that*.
> British English: The office which just opened in Beijing has been very successful.
> American English: The office that just opened in Beijing has been very successful.

This report provides an update on the Pitäkowski Water Treatment Plant project. The project requires building and installing a water treatment facility. The first report was issued in April and discussed work carried out during the first quarter. This report focuses on progress made during the second quarter. The second quarter included the months of April, May and June. Phase 1 was completed in early June. Phase 2 started in June. It is expected to end in September. Work is progressing well. Phase 2 includes equipment installation, pipe laying and construction oversight. These project steps will be described below.

. . . .

8 Decide whether each sentence delegates a task (d), compliments completed work or work in progress (c) or makes suggestions for carrying out work (s).

1. You should start by reviewing the information we've already received.
2. You did a great job. Thanks again for your help.
3. I'd appreciate it if you could send out the RFP.
4. I really appreciate your help.
5. Do you think you could help me out by setting up next week's conference call?
6. How about you start by contacting Samantha?
7. You might want to start by requesting the statistics from the Finance Department.
8. Thanks a lot. You really helped me out.
9. It might be good to start with researching our top competitor's recent developments.
10. I couldn't have done it without you. Thanks again!
11. I could really use your help.
12. I'm on a very tight schedule. Could you attend the 2 pm meeting in my place?

9 If a task has been delegated to you, it's often necessary to ask for clarification. Match the phrases that are similar in meaning.

1. When do you need it done by?
2. What should I start with?
3. Whom should I approach for information?
4. What's the best way to do that?
5. So you want me to …?

a. If I understand correctly, you'd like me to …?
b. What method do you suggest using?
c. What's the deadline?
d. In your opinion, what should be the priority, . . .
e. Can I talk to Aaron about it?

10 Listen to the dialogue and answer the questions. Which phrases are used to ...

🔊 22

delegate a task?

. . . .

. . . .

compliment Gerald?

. . . .

. . . .

. . . .

agree to handle a task?

. . . .

. . . .

clarify/confirm understanding of the task?

. . . .

. . . .

request the deadline?

. . . .

11 List three tasks that you would like to delegate to a colleague. Then delegate the tasks via email. Use relative clauses to provide important details about each task.

over to you

. . . .

. . . .

. . . .

. . . .

. . . .

. . . .

. . . .

. . . .

. . . .

. . . .

Unit checklist
- talk about products and services
- write a report
- brainstorm ideas
- discuss the benefits of professional communities

1 Find words from exercise 2 on page 126 of the coursebook that match the definitions.

1 more exclusive or expensive than products for the general public ....

2 including a large amount of space ....

3 extra items that go with a main item ....

4 clothing ....

5 financial support or another kind of support ....

6 to show that two things are not the same ....

2 Ling Chen summarizes a conversation with a client in an email. Listen and use 23 information from Ling's conversation to complete the email using reported speech.

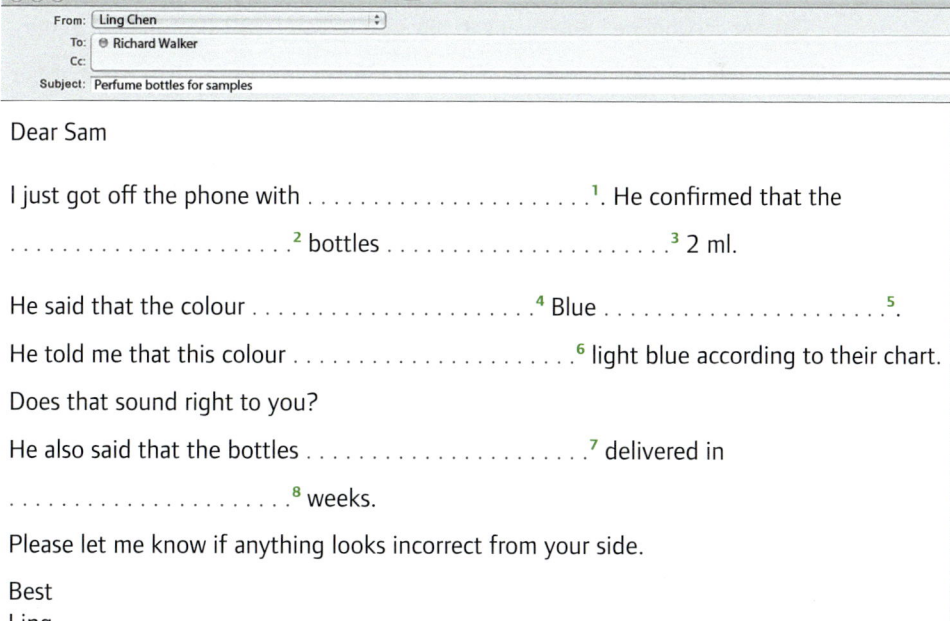

From: Ling Chen
To: Richard Walker
Cc:
Subject: Perfume bottles for samples

Dear Sam

I just got off the phone with ....¹. He confirmed that the

......................² bottles ....³ 2 ml.

He said that the colour ....⁴ Blue ....⁵.

He told me that this colour ....⁶ light blue according to their chart.

Does that sound right to you?

He also said that the bottles ....⁷ delivered in

......................⁸ weeks.

Please let me know if anything looks incorrect from your side.

Best
Ling

3 Two interviewers quickly discuss three job applicants. Complete the sentences with comparative or superlative forms using the words in the box.

> as (5x) • good (5x) • more (2x) • as much • than (3x) • young

Carole: Of the three people we interviewed, I think that Jessie is . . . . .¹ candidate. She has the experience we're looking for. She's also

. . . . .², so it's possible that she'll also try to build a long-term career here.

Kerry: Or she might decide to move on to a . . . . .³ position after only a few years. We're not able to offer a lot of money. And actually, I don't think we should consider age. What about James? He doesn't have

. . . . .⁴ experience . . . . .⁵ Jessie, but if we compare the two of them, he has a . . . . .⁶ education. His references are also outstanding.

Carole: Hmm. Jessie has . . . . .⁷ experience . . . . .⁸ James, but James has . . . . .⁹ qualifications . . . . .¹⁰ Jessie. What about Jacqueline? She seems to have . . . . .¹¹ personality, in my opinion. She falls somewhere between Jessie and James: It's true that her experience isn't . . . . .¹² extensive . . . . .¹³ Jessie's, and her qualifications aren't . . . . .¹⁴ outstanding . . . . .¹⁵ James', but I think she'd make an excellent team player. She's eager to learn and wants a long-term position.

Kerry: That's true. She definitely seemed to be . . . . .¹⁶ energetic

. . . . .¹⁷ both James and Jessie.

Carole: So let's call Jacqueline and offer her the job?

Kerry: I'll call her as soon as I get back to my office.

> **Tip** The word *information* is an uncountable mass noun and can never be plural in English. If you need to talk about incomplete information, use the word *piece* along with *information* to refer to one part or several parts.
> the information = all the information together; complete information
> a piece of information = one part of the information
>
> **A:** Did he give you the information?
> **B:** No, unfortunately not all of it, just a few pieces.

4 **Which section of a report (1–5) answers each question (a–i)? Put the questions in the correct sections. (Tip: For extra help, read through exercise 1 on page 129 of the coursebook.)**

a What does the report talk about?
b What can or should be done in the future?
c Were there any unexpected answers or pieces of information?
d Why should a future action be carried out?
e Why might the answers or test results be inaccurate?
f Who ordered the report?
g What is a recap of all the information presented in the report?
h What were the answers to the survey or what information was gathered?
i What is the goal of the report?

1 Terms of reference and introduction

....

....

....

2 Findings

....

....

3 Speculation

....

4 Conclusion

....

5 Recommendations

....

....

5 **In which section of a report would you use these phrases? Match the sections of a report (1–5 above) to the phrases (a–i).**

a We therefore recommend …   **f** It is advisable to …
b We discovered that …   **g** It was found that …
c It is possible that …   **h** In summary, …
d This report was requested by … **i** The aim of this report is to …
e We have been advised …

6 Complete the crossword puzzle using the transcript from track 2.22 on pages 203–204 of the coursebook.

1

2   3   4

5

6

7

8   9

Across
2 to fail
7 should (2 words)
8 maybe, possibly

Down
1 in contrast to (3 words)
3 a type of advertisement
4 a type of container that distributes or releases its contents
5 clearly, absolutely
6 a gift often used for marketing purposes
9 opinion, view, idea

7 Listen to a brainstorming session at a Canadian company and complete the mind-map with the ideas for promoting the new product. An extra line has been provided so that you can add an idea of your own.

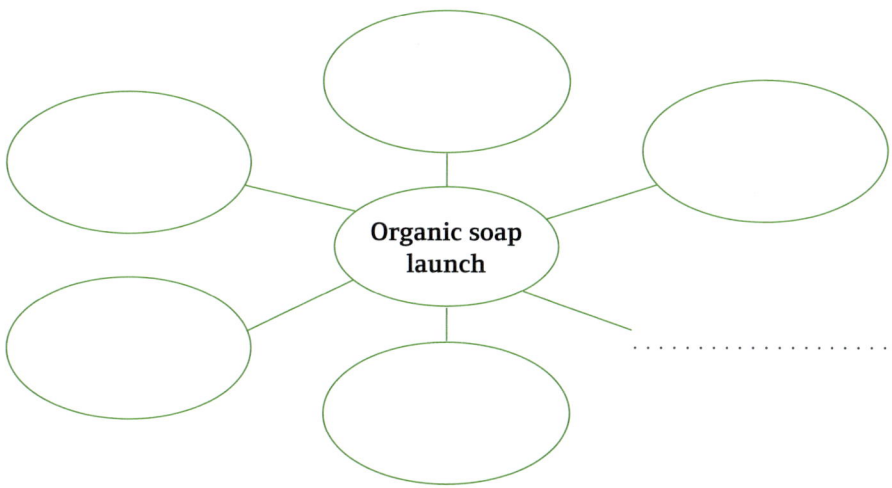

Organic soap launch

Did you know?

Always having an extra or "free" line on a mind-map while brainstorming helps people to come up with additional ideas.

8 Complete the questions and statements used to encourage a more open discussion of ideas. Listen again to check your answers.

1   Every idea is . . . . discussion, so . . . .
    hold back.

2   Okay, that's a good . . . .

3   Let's keep it . . . ., shall we?

4   Mmm. Interesting . . . .

5   Hmm. Wait a minute – . . . .? … I'm sure
    . . . . impossible.

6   You know, I . . . . that idea.

7   Are you . . . . about …?

8   Oh, yes, that's a . . . . suggestion.

9   Could you elaborate . . . . a bit?

9 **Find phrases in the text on page 132 of the coursebook to match the following definitions.**

1   to tell others about past situations and
    future possibilities   . . . .

2   forward movement within a particular sector   . . . .

3   to move from one piece of important online
    information to the next   . . . .

4   to make more connections with people and
    companies to benefit one's career   . . . .

5   to talk about tough issues   . . . .

6   a way of considering something that looks
    to the future   . . . .

10 **Before writing an entry in an online forum, it's important to analyse the contributions to assess the formality and tone. Read through some postings on your company's intranet or another professional online forum and complete the questionnaire.**

> **Writing style (tick Yes or No):**
> People use: **Yes   No**
>   complete sentences.   ☐   ☐
>   correct punctuation.   ☐   ☐
>   capitalization.   ☐   ☐
>
> **Vocabulary (circle the correct answer):**
> The vocabulary used in the posts is appropriate for people with:
>   **a basic/intermediate/advanced** understanding of English.
>   **technical knowledge / little or no technical knowledge**
>   about the subject.
>
> **Tone (circle the correct answer):**
> The attitude created through the posts is
>   **diplomatic and distant / friendly and open**.
>
> **Formality (tick Yes or No):**
> People respond to each other as if they are writing
> to their: **Yes   No**
>   potential clients or customers.   ☐   ☐
>   bosses.   ☐   ☐
>   coworkers.   ☐   ☐
>   coworkers with whom they have a friendly relationship. ☐ ☐
>   friends.   ☐   ☐

11 **Look at the websites mentioned on page 132 of the coursebook. Select one and write an appropriate professional profile of yourself using an analysis such as the one in exercise 10.**

over to you

✓ Progress check 3 → page 69

Check your knowledge from Units 1–3. Look at these questions (1–25) and tick the correct answer to each question. You get one point for each correct answer.

Personal information & experience   Points

1 "Jon's office is located in Hong Kong, …?" "Yes, I think so."
   a isn't he **b** or **c** isn't it **d** no
2 I speak German and English fluently, and I can … in Spanish and French.
   a go by **b** get by **c** pick up **d** contribute to
3 Nancy, do you have a minute? I'd like to … you to someone.
   a present **b** introduce **c** show **d** offer
4 Enrico, it was so nice … you again.
   a to see **b** hearing **c** meeting **d** to meet
5 "What do you do?" "I'm a team member, so I often … with my counterparts around the world."
   a set **b** lease **c** contact **d** liaise
6 I'll be an excellent team manager due to my ability to problem-solve and … my tasks.
   a prioritize **b** meet **c** improve **d** develop

Company facts   Points

7 Liane steps in wherever there's a problem with personnel. At the moment she … after the new interns in the operations department.
   a looks **b** is looking **c** sees **d** is seeing
8 "The company … consulting, does it?" "Well, yes, actually, it does."
   a isn't offering **b** doesn't offer **c** offers **d** hasn't offered
9 In the past we only focused on the financial sector. At the moment we're expanding … the services sector.
   a in **b** out of **c** from **d** into
10 We … active in the Asian market since 2008.
   a 've been **b** are **c** were **d** are being
11 Do we know who received the contract?" "No, we … notified yet.
   a aren't being **b** weren't **c** haven't been **d** aren't
12 In 2012, Ute Tannenbaum … to head our R&D department.
   a is hired **b** was hired **c** is hiring **d** is being hired

Emails & conference calls   **Points**

13 I'm sorry, but I'm writing to let you know that Mr Reynolds …
make it because of a double-booking with a meeting of the board of
directors. Is it possible to reschedule for next Tuesday?
  a shouldn't **b** must **c** can't **d** can

14 We look forward to … from you.
  a hearing **b** hear **c** getting **d** look

15 When will you kick … your next project?
  a in **b** up **c** off **d** over

16 Could you please let me know … Friday if you can make it?
  a until **b** through **c** up to **d** by

17 Francine sends her … She can't participate in the phone
conference today.
  a apologize **b** excuses **c** note **d** apologies

18 Sorry, I … that. We seem to have a bad connection. Could you
please repeat what you just said?
  a didn't listen to **b** didn't quite catch **c** 'm not hearing
  d am missing

19 No, I didn't know the offer was late. I promise I … it off now.
  a 'll send **b** am sending **c** 'll be sending **d** send

Small talk, discussing differences & team-building   **Points**

20 "…, I wanted to ask you when you're going on holiday." "Not until May."
  a On the side **b** By the way **c** Next to that
  d On the one side

21 I've heard a lot about it, but I've never been to Paris, … you?
  a were **b** are **c** will **d** have

22 It's important to gather … from employees after a team-building
activity in order to assess its success or failure.
  a teams **b** events **c** benefits **d** feedback

23 Susanne increased her … and overcame her fear during the activity.
  a distress **b** confidence **c** chances **d** limitations

24 We expected the employees of our partner company to have
professional … that were similar to ours, so we thought we'd meet
the project milestones on time.
  a characters **b** characteristics **c** incidents **d** traditions

25 Juan … the importance of the deadline by checking in with the
team leader at the end of every week.
  a assumed **b** underestimated **c** demonstrated
  d prevented

Total points: **/ 25**

Check your knowledge of Units 4–6. Look at these questions (1–25) and tick the correct answer to each question. You get one point for each correct answer.

Preventing & solving problems   Points

1 By … our suggestions, you'll be able to protect your equipment.
   a hearing   **b** following   **c** opening   **d** listening to

2 Have a good … strategy in order to avoid misplacing your possessions at an airport.
   a thinking   **b** open   **c** long-term   **d** mental

3 Always back … your computer system before travelling.
   a over   **b** down   **c** up   **d** through

4 If I … that preventative checks were included in the support package, I would have scheduled them every year.
   a knew   **b** was knowing   **c** know   **d** had known

5 "We need to improve our website." "I agree … to a point."
   a down   **b** up   **c** over   **d** through

6 As our brochure explains, we are standing by 24/7. If you … us, we'll be there.
   a don't need   **b** needed   **c** would need   **d** need

7 The delayed teleconference … a bad connection.
   a led to   **b** was due to   **c** resulted in   **d** made

8 At the last meeting, it was … that we should survey customers.
   a decided   **b** deciding   **c** found   **d** founding

Company information   Points

9 Their support packages are the … on the market, but are they comprehensive?
   a less expensive   **b** least expensive   **c** more expensive
   d most expensive

10 Our product is … those of our competitors.
   a so strong as   **b** as strong than   **c** as strong as
   d so strong than

11 We … specialize in financial planning, but now we also provide auditing services.
   a are used to   **b** used to   **c** using to   **d** had been using to

12 We're not able to provide the quantity. In … words, we don't have the capacity at this time.
   a other   **b** more   **c** different   **d** new

13 A successful retailer … a personalized relationship with customers.
   a sets up   **b** makes   **c** establishes   **d** grows

Presentations   Points

14 Now that I've reached the end of my presentation, I'd like to briefly … my main points.

    a readjust **b** recap **c** restart **d** return

15 To sum up my main point today: … you work with us, you'll get reliable, competent service.

    a when **b** while **c** because **d** whether

16 We'd like to discuss three points today, …, our history, our services and our client references.

    a therefore **b** whereas **c** namely **d** additionally

17 You can rely on us. Our team … to solving difficult technical issues.

    a is used **b** used **c** using **d** had been used

18 If I were you, I would … some slides for your presentation next week.

    a have prepared **b** prepared **c** prepare **d** preparing

19 Well, before I wrap things …, I'd like to make a final point.

    a over **b** down **c** around **d** up

Graphics   Points

20 To illustrate our market share in each major market, may I draw your attention … the next slide?

    a on **b** onto **c** to **d** in

21 As you can see, our market share was increasing when it suddenly … to only 10 per cent.

    a fall **b** had fallen **c** was falling **d** fell

22 If we add these two … of the pie chart together, we can see that most of our budget goes to production and marketing.

    a trends **b** segments **c** circles **d** lines

23 The chart shows that the market is expected to grow … fast over the next five years.

    a extremely **b** amazing **c** sudden **d** suddenly

24 I'm very sorry that the computer projector has stopped working. After our lunch break, I'll have some … of the charts and graphs for you.

    a freebies **b** giveaways **c** handouts

    d emergency backups

25 Could you please create a …? We need to illustrate our company history and indicate the most important milestones.

    a bar chart **b** timeline **c** pie chart **d** flow chart

Total points: **/ 25**

Check your knowledge of Units 7–10. Look at these questions (1–25) and tick the correct answer to each question. You get one point for each correct answer.

Negotiating   Points

1 Please … in mind that we would like to establish a long-term relationship with you.
   a have **b** bare **c** bear **d** hold

2 I'm afraid we can't consider your proposal as it … It's too risky for us.
   a stands **b** is standing **c** stood **d** has stood

3 In light of new information, we'll have to … the current offer.
   a turn down **b** contribute **c** point out **d** suggest

4 I hope we can … a consensus before the end of today's session.
   a get **b** reach **c** see **d** make

5 We agree to the amount, but we'd like you to modify your terms and …
   a quantity **b** quality **c** conditions **d** counteroffer

6 I've run out of ideas. Can you … a solution?
   a bring up **b** point out **c** make **d** suggest

7 …, we've agreed on the quantity and price. What about the guarantee?
   a Until this morning **b** So far **c** Tomorrow **d** Yesterday

Making requests & delegating   Points

8 I asked him to help me with the employee performance assessments next week, but he told me he … for vacation on Friday.
   a leaves **b** is leaving **c** was leaving **d** will leave

9 I'd appreciate it if you … attend the conference in May, as it will be extremely important for establishing new contacts.
   a can **b** cannot **c** could **d** couldn't

10 "How should I begin?" "You should start … Susanna. She handled it last year."
   a by asking **b** to ask **c** up with **d** over with

11 Effective delegation requires giving someone the … to carry out the job however he or she wants.
   a expectation **b** desire **c** faith **d** freedom

12 "What did he say when you asked him to take over the arrangements?" "Well, he said he … know if he would have the time."
   a doesn't **b** didn't **c** won't **d** wouldn't

13 I'd really appreciate it if you … tell me how many employees will be affected by the restructuring.
   a can **b** will **c** could **d** wouldn't

Company decisions

14 Every decision in business has a trade-…, so it's very important for us to weigh the costs and benefits of the proposal.
    a   on   **b**   over   **c**   off   **d**   after

15 To keep up with our competitors, we'll need to … our network quickly.
    a   expedite   **b**   expand   **c**   open   **d**   close

16 Of course all employees are invited to the team-building weekend! Your invitation … have been misplaced.
    a   must   **b**   mustn't   **c**   could   **d**   couldn't

17 Willi said he's decided to move production abroad? That would affect more than half of our employees. He … be serious!
    a   mightn't   **b**   must   **c**   could't   **d**   can't

18 During the next two months, the board of directors … whether to open new branches.
    a   decide   **b**   are deciding   **c**   will have decided
    d   will be deciding

Projects

19 "I can't deliver the statistics by next week." "So what … is that you need more time?"
    a   you've said   **b**   you've been saying   **c**   you say
    d   you're saying

20 "What will they … by the end of next week?" "Most likely Phase 4."
    a   be completing   **b**   have completed   **c**   be working
    d   have worked

21 She thought her request for information had been clear, so she was … by the answer from her colleague.
    a   excited   **b**   confused   **c**   fascinated   **d**   delighted

22 "What are the project's …?" "A report and a plan of action."
    a   milestones   **b**   deliverables   **c**   objects   **d**   supplies

23 The person … responsible for determining the budget is extremely competent.
    a   who's   **b**   whose   **c**   that is   **d**   which is

24 "What's the status of the project in Utrecht?" "It's … schedule. We're very pleased."
    a   upon   **b**   over   **c**   on   **d**   in

25 "How do the numbers look?" "Unfortunately we're … budget by $2 million."
    a   at   **b**   under   **c**   within   **d**   over

Total points: **/ 25**

Answer key

1 1 provides   4 aim
2 are looking   5 are doing research
3 includes   6 are increasing

2

Simple present	Present continuous
every day	at the moment
always	currently
usually	at present
sometimes	right now

3 *Example:*
Good morning, ladies and gentlemen. My name is Frank Müller, and I'm the director of R&D at MG Stahl, a large steel manufacturer based in southern Germany. MG Stahl provides steel pipes and other steel parts to companies in many sectors. Currently, we are working on …

4 1 In Atlanta?   3 aren't you?
2 doesn't it? /   4 Some old
   Recycling services?   acquaintances?

5 1 b, **2** a, **3** a, **4** b, **5** b, **6** a

6 1 at, **2** for, **3** on, **4** of, **5** for, **6** with, **7** to, **8** to, **9** in

Collocations:
at the conference   work closely with
filling in for   reports to
on leave   report to
in charge of   interested in
perfect for

7 1 is made, is making
2 is updated
3 is attending
4 is being prepared, feel

8 1 is made   5 is removed
2 is used   6 are being made
3 are being opened   7 are added
4 are cleaned   8 is being put

9 1 e or f, **2** a, **3** d, **4** e or f, **5** b, **6** c

1 hierarchical structure
2 individual responsibility
3 flexible structure
4 production costs
5 inventory management
6 hands-on approach

10 1 We don't have a formal chain of command.
2 It's important for our company strategy to be flexible.
3 We encourage our employees to expand their scope of responsibility.
4 Salaries are decided by both associates and supervisors.
5 Our product range includes components for the electronics industry.

The company being described is W. L. Gore & Associates.

11 1 bureaucratic   5 independent
2 compensation   6 initiative
3 corporate   7 production/productive
4 flexible   8 to rank

12 *Example:*
I work for a large pharmaceutical company. In 2011, the company was ranked as the best pharmaceutical company to work for if you have children. It offers flexible work hours. Our supervisors expect us to take personal initiative to …

1

Formal emails	Informal emails
with reference to please accept my apologies I will be unable to attend Dear due to I regret to inform you	I can't make it sorry again because of it's about I'm sorry, but Hi

2
1 's been (has been)
2 for
3 have been going
4 since
5 took
6 four weeks ago
7 two days ago
8 ordered
9 was
10 has been offering
11 since
12 weren't
13 had
14 gets

The email is informal. You can tell because the writer uses language such as "hi" and the topic of the email is presented informally to a colleague.

3
1 Did you have to worry about your online image 20 years ago?
2 What is everywhere?
3 Since when has HideAway been managing online information for people?
4 Who has HideAway helped?
5 Who decides what information stays and what goes?
6 Why do you need HideAway?

4
1 Designed by You was founded by fashion students Samantha Richards and Kara Mendez in 2009.
2 The clothing is made by Designed by You.
3 Then the clothing is sent to the customer (by Designed by You).
4 the company's first store was opened in California in 2011.
5 The original website was expanded (by Designed by You) in 2012.
6 Customers' clothing lines are marketed to different clothing stores (by Designed by You).

5 1 c, **2** e, **3** d, **4** a, **5** b, **6** c

6 *Example:*
1 I love it. Not too big and not too small. Where do you live?
2 We hired about 10 new employees last year. How large is your company?
3 It's great we can sit outside. Have you ever been to this restaurant before?
4 But I've read a few of his articles. Where have you heard him speak?
5 It's always a good choice! How is your pasta?

6 I prefer Formula 1™. Have you ever seen a live race?

7 U: Good morning, you must be Tamara.
T: Ulrike, good morning. It's a pleasure to meet you in person.
U: Nice to meet you, too. Did you have any trouble finding the restaurant?
T: None at all, thanks for asking. It is very conveniently located.
U: I guess we should try to order right away. It can get very busy here.
T: Good idea. Do you have any suggestions?
U: Well, during business meetings I always order the English breakfast.
T: Sounds great. I'll have the English breakfast and a large black coffee.
U: So, have you been to Köln before?
T: No, this is my first visit. Well, this is the first visit during which I'll have time to look around.
U: It's great that the weather is a little warmer today.
T: Really? Well then, I'll have to consider myself lucky.
U: What are you planning to see while you're here?
T: I'm not sure. What do you recommend?
U: Well, I'd start by.... Oh, here comes the waiter for our order.

8 *Example:*
To learn about someone's current personal and professional activities:
1 a, 2 a, 3 b, 4 a, 5 b, 7 b, 8 a, 9
To only learn about a new work situation:
1b, 6b, 2b, 7b, 8a, 9 (but note that by following this path, important information about the company's recent acquisition [box 5] isn't given)

9
1 face-to-face contact
2 communication breakdown
3 sources of possible conflict
4 case study
5 mutual respect
6 to increase (someone's) sensitivity to/toward
7 project milestones
8 on an ongoing basis
1 f, **2** t, **3** f, **4** f

10 *Example:*

Dear Mr Sánchez

Congratulations on your new job here at RollerWorld. My name is Yolanda Ebert and I'm looking forward to meeting you. I work in R&D as a project manager, so we are in the same department and have the same job, but I have a different team leader.

Mr Schreiber asked me to get in contact with you before you begin regarding policies at our company. There are three aspects of doing business in Germany that I'd like to tell you more about: using formal titles with colleagues, being on time, and meeting with business partners outside of the office.

First, people in Germany use formal titles such as Dr, Mr or Ms plus a person's surname to address each other, even if they work together and have known each other for a long time. In general, first names aren't used. If someone has a higher position than you do, always address that person with a formal title unless they offer you their first name.

Second, it's very important to come to meetings on time.

Third, we encourage staff, especially team leaders and project managers, to meet with business partners outside of the office on an ongoing basis so that they have face-to-face contact and are able to build mutual respect. You will have access to a credit card you'll be able to use for these meetings.

I'll inform you more about these guidelines when we meet in a few weeks. I look forward to working with you!

Sincerely
Yolanda Ebert

Unit 3 pages 17–22

1 1 d, 're going to
   2 a, 'll (will) be able to
   3 b, 'll (will) do
   4 c, 're (are) going to
   5 a, 'll (will) accept (note that 'we're offering' describes a current action and is present continuous)
   6 c, 'm going to

2 1 'm going to prepare
   2 'll need
   3 'm going to meet, I'm meeting
   4 'll send, 'm going to send
   5 're going to talk, 're talking
   6 'll meet, 're going to meet, 're meeting

3 1 a, **2** a, **3** a, **4** a or b, **5** a or b, **6** a or b, **7** b, **8** a, **9** a, **10** a or b, **11** a, **12** a

4 1 f, The first point is the topics that should be covered during the training.
   2 f, The aspects to consider are the point of sale equipment and effectively handling the computer and phone systems.
   3 t
   4 n
   5 t

   1 didn't quite catch that
   2 just come in here
   3 Sorry to interrupt
   4 just going to say
   5 could cut in

5 1 <u>15</u> offers have been received and evaluated
   2 vendors <u>haven't been</u> selected
   3 orders will be placed <u>tomorrow</u>
   4 Glen <u>will send</u> it in an email

6 1 Have you already made the travel arrangements?
   2 Have we received the invitation to tender yet?
   3 Have you had lunch yet?
   4 Have we already gotten feedback from the client?

7 *Example:*

Hi Dave

We wanted to send you an update on the construction project. We've already called the supplier and they've agreed to our terms and conditions. Nothing has been signed yet, but we're consulting with our legal department.

We've already contacted the local authorities. The documents we need before we can start the work haven't arrived yet, but we expect to get them by the end of the week.

Best
Chuck

8 *Example:*
1 Stephanie's answer focuses more on professional information and her skills and experience.
2 Ryan's answer provides concrete examples of his qualities. He also says something positive about the quality of the company's products.
3 Stephanie sounds more goal-focused and willing to accept challenges than Ryan.
4 Ryan gives concrete examples; Stephanie's answer is so short it seems that the opposite might be true.
5 The interviewer might not like Stephanie's answer; if Stephanie is hired she might become competition for the interviewer! As an alternative, Stephanie could say "I'd like to have a job like yours." This alternative answer would be less threatening to the interviewer. Ryan's answer is more flexible, but some interviewers might find it to be too flexible – it might appear that he doesn't know what he wants or doesn't have any specific professional goals.
6 In some countries, the interviewer's question is illegal. Each answer represents a different way of dealing with it.

9 1 c, **2** f, **3** e, **4** b, **5** d, **6** a

1 relevant experience
2 best candidate
3 track record
4 interesting question
5 ambitious goal
6 team member

10 *Example:*
1 when used in this way: to relax
2 to give
3 to be appropriate for
4 to lose control
5 to be worried
6 when used in this way: to successfully deal with a problem or negative situation
'to freak out' is an informal term

11 1 e, **2** a, **3** b, **4** f, **5** c, **6** d

12 *Example:*
2 We can listen and pay attention to team members who aren't team leaders.

3 We can think of new ideas when we are outside in nature.
4 We can brainstorm in a new environment to find different solutions.
5 Team members can take on new roles.
6 We can improve our cooperation with each other.

Unit 4 pages 23-28

1 1 readjust
2 standing by
3 malfunction
4 field visit
5 preventative check
6 service technician
7 remote
8 sound advice

2 1 cause: a mistake by the machine operator; effect: expensive repair bill
A mistake by the machine operator (has) led to an expensive repair bill.
2 cause: the client got lost in the city; effect: the meeting started late
The client got lost in the city, so the meeting started late.
3 cause: successful launch of a top-selling product; effect: an increase in stock prices
Last quarter we successfully launched a top-selling product. As a result of this, the company experienced an increase in stock prices.
4 cause: an increase in gasoline prices; effect: an increase in delivery costs
An increase in gasoline prices has caused an increase in delivery costs.
5 cause: a storm over the Atlantic; effect: a three-hour flight delay
A storm over the Atlantic meant a three-hour flight delay.
6 cause: technical problems; effect: the conference call was postponed
The conference call was postponed due to technical problems.

3 1 As, arrived
2 before, was checking / before, had checked
3 recommended, after
4 got, while

Past continuous	Past perfect
as	before
when	after
while	–

4
1	was checking	7	had saved
2	stopped	8	deleted
3	said	9	was talking
4	didn't send,	10	rang
	hadn't sent	11	had promised
5	failed	12	has been
6	had made		

5 1 t, 2 f, 3 f, 4 f, 5 t, 6 t

  1 Let me make sure that I've understood you
    correctly.
  2 Just to summarize:

6 *Example:*
Dear Ms Smith-Böhm

Thank you for talking with me this morning about the possible job. The following is a brief summary of our conversation.

I would like to offer you a temporary early shift warehouse manager job starting Monday at a company located in the southeastern part of the city. The company produces plastic components for cars. Most of the staff are foreign, so it will be necessary to communicate in English.

The contract is attached. Please sign it and send it to me via mail, fax, or email.

Sincerely

Renate Müller
Personal Plus

7 1 To be honest, I really disagree / Well, that
    could be true
  2 I'm not so sure about that / I think it's a
    good idea
  3 I'm not convinced that … will work
  4 Sounds good
  5 I'm sorry to disagree, but I don't think
    that will work
  6 Unfortunately I have to disagree

Strongly disagree	Neutral opinion	Strongly agree
6　5　1　3	2　1	2　4

Note that answers will vary.

8 1 Our strategy needs to be reevaluated. The
    clients can't be expected to contact us.
  2 The clients must be contacted immediately
    after the service is carried out.
  3 Our databases should be improved to
    better track this information.
  4 Updates about our progress must be
    given/submitted on a weekly basis. /
    I need to be updated about our progress
    on a weekly basis.

  6 Mr Lopez from the M&A department is to
    give an update. / The mergers &
    acquisitions department update is to be
    given by Mr Lopez.

10 Across   **Down**

	Across		Down
1	impart	2	appoint
3	unbiased	4	allocate
6	bond	5	assumption
9	succinct	7	consensus
10	productive	8	acronym
11	grudge		

Unit 5 pages 29-34

1 *Example:*
Project engineers
To learn about the new health insurance plan
Only as employees who receive health insurance; no HR knowledge of the topic
Engineering degrees, mostly diplomas
30-45

9 2 It was shown/has been shown that all
    current staff are overworked and that
    their satisfaction is low.
  3 It was decided/has been decided (by the
    board) to increase staff by 10 per cent by
    May of next year.
  4 It was decided/has been decided (by the
    board) to distribute profits to shareholders
    by the third quarter.
  5 The Finance Committee is to present the
    current status of investments.

Mostly male
Mixed: German, Chinese and Canadian

2 1 'll offer, start
2 don't do top work, will be negatively affected
3 is dissatisfied, will make it
4 start in two weeks, 'll give you a 20% bonus
5 don't accept, will you change your decision

3 1 didn't start
2 would
3 would
4 talked
5 were
6 'd/would accept
7 were
8 'd/would say
9 'll/will be
10 want

4 *Example:*
Yes, I would take Steffen's advice. If I were Josef, I would take the job, even if I burned a bridge with my current company. It's very important to me to advance in my career.

5 1 had known
2 would you have changed
3 had told
4 would have thought
5 had known
6 would it have changed
7 had known
8 would have ordered

6 a 7, b 4, c 1, d 8, e 3, f 6, g 5, h 2

7 *Example:*
2 Fact: RollerWorld is a trusted partner for all your inline skating needs. We've been ranked as the top supplier five years in a row by Inline magazine.
Rhetorical question: Why should you trust us?
Anecdote: The last time I was here to speak with you, the head of your design department made a very interesting point …
3 Fact: Germany offers vacation activities for all members of the family.
Rhetorical question: Germany is known for its beer gardens, but did you know that 14 national parks are within its borders?

Anecdote: My 16-year-old niece visited us last year. We went to museums and parks.
4 Fact: Our town offers multiple financial benefits for companies that want to set up their headquarters or a branch office here.
Rhetorical question: Did you know that our town offers you access to the resources and infrastructure needed for success in business today?
Anecdote: Two years ago, a young woman from Ohio set up her business here …

8 *Example:*
2 In other words, if you want to work with qualified, professional service that's available 24/7 and helps you save money on equipment costs, you should work with us.
3 So, by choosing electric cars, you can save money and the environment, and you can improve your company's image.
4 In sum, if you want to provide easy access for your employees and clients, save money on energy costs, and design your office space to fit you and your company, reserve your space today!

9 1 e, 2 f, 3 d, 4 b, 5 a, 6 c

1 extensive network
2 personalized relationship
3 significant factor
4 emerging market

10 1 That was a brief overview of our financial services.
2 To conclude, let me just review the main points.
3 That brings me to the end of my presentation today.
4 That just about wraps things up.
5 I hope that's given you some idea of our services.

11 1 acknowledgment
2 to commit
3 to congratulate
4 to gratify
5 to identify
6 imagination
7 temptation
8 trick
9 satisfaction

1 1 c, **2** d, **3** f, **4** a

Flow chart: a process such as a manufacturing or approval process
Table: data that must be presented using exact figures or details so that one can easily see changes or differences between two or more years or scenarios; financial summaries that show two years are often presented in tables

2 *Example:*
The purpose of the graphic is clearer for the audience in the first description.
The connection to the audience is unclear in the second description.
The first description of the changes in the chart gives the audience enough time to follow and understand the changes.

In principle, the first description is more effective for the audience because it 1) introduces the graphic and its purpose before showing it; 2) clearly explains how the subject connects to the audience and the goal of showing the graphic to the audience; and 3) defines and describes the graphic step by step, allowing the audience enough time to process the information.

3 *Example:*
1 Vietnam has the highest population.
Of the three countries, Mongolia's population is the lowest.
Compared to Germany and Mongolia, Vietnam has the greatest population.
Mongolia's population is much lower than Vietnam's or Germany's.
Germany's population is almost as large as Vietnam's.
2 Mongolia's GDP per capita is higher than Vietnam's.
Vietnam has a lower GDP per capita than Mongolia.
3 Ireland has a higher GDP per capita than Germany.
Germany's GDP per capita is lower than Ireland's.
4 Germany's unemployment rate is lower than Ireland's.

Ireland has a higher unemployment rate than Germany.

4 1 f, **2** e, **3** a, **4** b, **5** d, **6** a, **7** c

5 Moving on, let's look at Namibia. Our sales have been steadily increasing in Namibia since entering the market there three years ago. Our competitors have decided to leave the country entirely, whereas we have chosen to increase our sales efforts there. Since our competitors are leaving, I know it might appear as if our success will be easy. Nonetheless, we need to continue our focused marketing efforts and launch products specifically tailored to customers in the country. Therefore/Consequently, today I'd like to propose adapting three of our top-selling products in South Africa for the Namibian market. Moreoever, I'd also like to propose reviewing the products that are already selling very well in Namibia to ensure that they are meeting the needs of the buyers 100 per cent. Therefore/Consequently, we'll need to develop product assessment methods specific to the Namibian market. Well, those are our rather ambitious plans for Namibia. Now let's turn to our rather poor performance in Kenya.

6 1 a, **2** b, **3** b, **4** b, **5** a, **6** a

Rules:
Present: to be, verb-ing
to be, verb-ing
Past: infinitive
did, infinitive

7 1 Did Jenny use to attend the trade fairs?
2 OfficePro didn't use to be the top-selling product.
3 Did Ravi use to work for your company?
4 Is Jose used to making field visits?
5 Our competitors are used to having low sales in Namibia.
6 Matthew is not used to living in a country with such cold weather.

8 1 Can we come back to that later?
2 Sorry, I don't know the answer to that but I will find out.

3 I see what you mean. / Oh, that's a good question.
4 I see what you mean. / Oh, that's a good question.
5 Oh, that's a good question. / I see what you mean.
6 Can we come back to that later?

9
1 confidential data
2 lost and found
3 airport contractors
4 departure gate
5 security checkpoint
6 retail establishment
7 airport personnel
8 stupid mistakes
9 mental strategy
10 security measures

10 *Example:*
The first graphic I'd like to bring your attention compares the weekly frequency of laptop loss for four European airports. Since you are all businesspeople who travel throughout Europe, we'd like to make you aware of these rates so you can see why our travel insurance for top managers is so valuable. Here you can see that the losses in London, at 900 per week, is by far the highest. Next comes Amsterdam and Paris, which are both between 700 and 750. At 300 per week, Frankfurt's rate is the lowest. But we think that even 300 lost laptops per week is high, and we don't want you and your data to be at risk. That takes me to my next point: how our travel insurance protects you and your company.

Unit 7 pages 41-46

1
1 suppose
2 be better
3 be interested
4 can't consider
5 be open
6 may not

2
1 And what would you be interested in at the moment?
2 Might you also be open to a slightly different proposal?
3 I'm afraid we can't consider such a large quantity at the moment.
4 Well, I suppose things may change.

3 **Rules:** simple past; past continuous; tell; if or whether
1 He said that the team leader was extremely competent.
2 She told (me/him/her/them/us) that the legal department wasn't reviewing the contract.
3 She wanted to know if/whether he went to the committee meetings.

4 **Rules:** past perfect; past perfect continuous; do not; warn
1 He warned (me/us) that they had wanted to talk with (me/us) about the late delivery.
2 She said that she hadn't checked her email all day.
3 He wondered if/whether they had been working on the strategic plan.
4 They noted that before it had risen in 2009, it had plummeted to $10.36 per share.

5 **Rules:** do change; do not change
1 She asked me/us if I/we wouldn't see him at the trade fair in August.
2 He said that we could forget about catching our flight.
3 He wondered why we wouldn't export to Mongolia. He said that consumption was soaring at the moment.
4 She pointed out that the task force should set clear priorities.

6 **Rules:** does not change
1 They say that their workshops promote teamwork.
2 The committee insists that incentives aren't enough to motivate employees.
3 She says that they weren't able to convince them to accept the offer.

7 1 e, **2** c, **3** a, **4** b, **5** f, **6** d

8 *Example:*
Their representative said that they couldn't decrease the price.
Frank said that he wanted …
We asked them …
Anna said that …

9 **1** at least five
   2 the increase in gas prices and the company's efforts to promote itself as a green company
   3 five electric cars for 25,000 Euro each
   4 18,000 Euro per electric car
   5 to buy a mix of electric cars and conventional cars: three electric cars for 25,000 Euro each instead of five electric cars, and two conventional cars with excellent fuel efficiency at 19,000 Euro each
   6 the profit margin is too low
   7 one conventional car for 18,000 Euro and four electric cars for 21,000 Euro; the warranty on the three electric-powered cars will be increased from three to five years

Tentative language:
We were thinking that we would need …
We were thinking of using …
Do you think we could work something out?
We could offer you …
we were hoping for …
We really couldn't agree to that at the moment.
Maybe I could put forward another idea?
Suppose we were to offer you …
I might be able to argue for … if you were willing to …
Could you give us …

10 **1** to form a strategic partnership
   2 to maintain good relationships
   3 to set parameters
   4 to give someone room
   5 to get impatient with someone
   6 to know the breakdown

Unit 8 pages 47-52

1 **1** frustrated **8** embarrassing
   2 confused **9** enthusiastic
   3 furious **10** fascinating
   4 annoying **11** stunning
   5 irritated **12** delighted
   6/7 puzzled/surprised

2 **1** She must be teleworking today.
   2 The office gossip simply can't be true!
   3 She must be wondering why we've offered so many concessions.

4 Could he be joking?
5 He must be impressed by your sales skills.
6 Might they be a little frustrated?

3 **1** He could have asked
   2 They must have been meeting
   3 She might not have heard
   4 Could they have been looking; That might have been
   5 Might she have been waiting

4 Hans Meyer
East Coast Regional Manager
Two more offices will be opened by the end of next year
Company is in the US market because the waste disposal industry is growing and is still open to new competitors
In business: 15 years
Entered the Eastern European market five years ago
Concerns: none
Equipment recycles plastic
Idea developed in Germany: recycling standards are high

Open questions:
1 Why did your company decide to set up a branch here?
2 What concerns do you have that your technology will become outdated in favor of technology and materials that are more environmentally friendly?
3 How did the idea develop?

Closed questions:
1 Could I just confirm that your name is Hans Meyer?
2 And your title is East Coast Regional Manager?
3 Would you mind if I threw this in your trash can?
4 And you supply machinery that's used in the production of plastic?
5 So do you see yourselves as part of the future of plastic?

5 **1** How do you plan to deal with seasonal factors?
   2 What would be the advantage of postponing the negotiation?

3 Could you consider a hypothetical situation for a moment?

4 When would it be possible for you to give us a rough estimate?

5 Why do you think we're struggling to reach a consensus?

6 Shall we persuade Sam to join the new office?

6 **Asking for your business partner's opinion:**
I'd like to hear your perspective.
Can you suggest a solution?
Restating or affirming your partner's position or perspective:
I understand your position.
I understand your concern.
So you're saying that …
Explaining / Offering a suggestion / Voicing an opinion or concern:
How about doing something different?
Perhaps it would be a good idea to …
I'm afraid there's another issue …
Can I explain how I see things from my perspective?
You probably didn't realize that …

7 **1** Can you suggest a solution? / I'd like to hear your perspective.
2 you probably didn't realize that
3 So you're saying that
4 Perhaps it would be a good idea to
5 I understand your position. / I understand your concern.
6 I'm afraid there's another issue.
7 I understand your position / I understand your concern
8 How about doing something different?

8 *Example:*
In Germany it's very important to be on time for appointments, but at my company the staff is over 50% international and it's very common for meetings to start late.

Unit 9 pages 53-58

1 **1** The name of the radio show is Environmental Earth.
2 true
3 true

4 In the past, <u>chlorine</u> has been used to disinfect water.
5 UV <u>can't</u> always be used to disinfect water.

2 **1** , replacing Mona Redmond
2 , ensuring that we stick to the budget and meet tight deadlines
3 , so we each need to make an extra effort to make sure that we
4 As a result,
5 directly via email or phone
6 Unless anyone has any objections or time conflicts,

3 **1** to work collaboratively
2 to show initiative
3 go through a process
4 to maintain communication
5 to encounter problems
6 to fall through at the last moment
7 to work on a tight schedule

Phrases in 2 with similar meanings
to work on a tight schedule – meet tight deadlines
to work collaboratively – always work together
to show initiative – to take action
to encounter problems – any issue that comes up
to maintain communication – to stay in touch

4 **Rules:** will be; will have
1 will have completed
2 will you be dealing
3 we'll be designing
4 (we'll be) communicating with
5 will be procuring
6 we'll have completed
7 we'll have started
8 won't have finished

Prepositions that signal a cutoff date or deadline in the future: by, within
Prepositions or relative adverbs of time that signal an ongoing period: for, during, while

5 **1** d; The client <u>who called yesterday</u> complimented our new service plan.
2 n; Aweco's CEO, <u>who was at the trade fair in Frankfurt</u>, will be in town next Wednesday.

3 d; The man whose computer was stolen at the airport is employed by our biggest competitor.

4 d; The financial report that was issued yesterday included three interesting ideas for increasing our profit margin.

5 n; Version 2.0 of the technical manual, which was written by Erik, describes the functions in more detail than past versions.

6 1 b, **2** a, **3** a

7 *Example:*
This report provides an update on the Pitäkowski Water Treatment Plant project, which requires building and installing a water treatment facility.
This report focuses on progress made during the second quarter, which includes (the months of) April, May and June.
Phase 2, which started in June, is expected to end in September. / Phase 2, which is expected to end in September, started in June.
The steps in Phase 2, which include equipment installation, pipe laying and construction oversight, will be described below. / The steps that make up Phase 2, equipment installation, pipe laying and construction oversight, will be described below.

8 **1** s, **2** c, **3** d, **4** c, **5** d, **6** s, **7** s, **8** c, **9** s, **10** c, **11** d, **12** d

9 **1** c, **2** d, **3** e, **4** b, **5** a

10 **To delegate a task:**
I wanted to ask you if you could help me out with something.
Do you think you could work on the sales projections?

To compliment Gerald:
I know how much you enjoy...
Every time you've stepped in...you've done an excellent job.
That's be great! Thanks a ton. You're really helping me out.

To agree to handle a task:
Sure, Patrizia, I'd be happy to.
No problem. I'll get right on it.

To clarify/confirm understanding of the task:
Just to confirm, though, you need me to work on the sales projections for each car line? Okay. Only the two luxury lines.

To request the deadline:
And by when do you need them?

11 Dealing with phone calls, responding to phone messages, taking meeting minutes
Example:

Dear Marc

At the moment I'm extremely busy and I was wondering if you could help me out. Every day I get about 10 phone calls or messages from clients who are both new and international. These clients, who usually call between 8 and 10 am, often want information that you could easily provide to them as well. I know how much you enjoy dealing with clients who want to build long-term relationships with us. Would you mind if I forwarded the calls to you? It would really appreciate it.

We could see how it works out and then reevaluate after a month. Sound okay to you?

Best
Nico

Unit 10 pages 59-64

1 **1** upscale **4** apparel
2 extensive **5** sponsorship
3 accessories **6** differentiate

2 **1** Richard **5** 508
2 20,000 **6** was
3 would hold **7** would be
4 was **8** three

3 **1** the best **10** than
2 the youngest **11** the best
3 better **12** as
4 as much **13** as
5 as **14** as
6 better **15** as
7 more **16** more
8 than **17** than
9 better

4 **1** **Terms of reference and introduction:**
    a What does the report talk about?
    f Who ordered the report?
    i What is the goal of the report?
  2 **Findings:**
    c Were there any unexpected answers or pieces of information?
    h What were the answers to the survey or what information was gathered?
  3 **Speculation:**
    e Why might the answers or test results be inaccurate?
  4 **Conclusion:**
    g What is a recap of all information presented?
  5 **Recommendations:**
    b What can or should be done in the future?
    d Why should a future action be carried out?

5 **a** 5, **b** 2, **c** 3, **d** 1, **e** 2, **f** 5, **g** 2, **h** 4, **i** 1

6 **Across**
  2 flop
  7 supposed to
  8 potentially

  Down
  1 as opposed to
  3 promotion
  4 dispenser
  5 expressly
  6 freebie
  9 input

7 advertising in the store's weekly product brochure
offer a freebie
let customers try a sample in the store
online promotions
direct mail

8 **1** open for;
    please don't
  2 start
  3 in mind
  4 idea

  5 why not; it's not
  6 really like
  7 talking
  8 very good
  9 on that

9 **1** to share experiences and ideas
  2 advances in (an) industry
  3 to follow relevant links
  4 to expand a professional network
  5 to discuss challenges
  6 forward thinking

10 Answers will depend on the intranet or forum
11 *Example:*
I offer consulting services to companies that want to …
I am looking for new contacts who …
My interests include …

Progress Check 1 Unit 1-3

Personal information & experience
1 c, **2** b, **3** b, **4** a, **5** d, **6** a

Company facts
7 b, **8** b, **9** d, **10** a, **11** c, **12** b

Emails & conference calls
13 c, **14** a, **15** c, **16** d, **17** d, **18** b, **19** a

Small talk, discussing differences & team-building
20 b, **21** d, **22** d, **23** b, **24** b, **25** c

Progress Check 2 Unit 4-6

Preventing & solving problems
1 b, **2** d, **3** c, **4** d, **5** b, **6** d, **7** b, **8** a

Company information
9 b, **10** c, **11** b, **12** a, **13** c

Presentations
14 b, **15** a, **16** c, **17** a, **18** c, **19** d

Graphics
20 c, **21** d, **22** b, **23** a, **24** c, **25** b

Progress Check 3 Unit 7-10

Negotiating
1 c, **2** a, **3** a, **4** b, **5** c, **6** d, **7** b

Making requests & delegating
8 c, **9** c, **10** a, **11** d, **12** b, **13** c

Company decisions
14 c, **15** b, **16** a, **17** d, **18** d

Projects
19 d, **20** b, **21** b, **22** b, **23** a, **24** c, **25** d

Transcripts

Unit 1

Exercise 1

Good afternoon, ladies and gentlemen. My name is Roger Winsted, Chairman of Richmond Consultants LLP, and I am delighted to be giving the keynote address at this year's LeMaNe conference here in Poland. Before I begin, let me tell you a little bit about the consulting firm I represent. Richmond Consultants is a global firm that provides consultation services to companies that are looking for ways to optimize their logistics or solve logistics problems. Our client portfolio includes Fortune 500 companies as well as start-ups. Our company motto is "Start at 30". This means that whatever the problem, we aim for an improvement of at least 30 per cent.

This is a very exciting year for us. Together with a university partner, we are doing research on a new concept that depends 100 per cent on robots in warehouses and logistics centres. Furthermore, we are increasing our presence in the Middle East.

But now let's turn to our main theme, the focus of this year's conference …

Exercise 4

1   A: Where are you based?
    B: I'm based in Chicago, but right now I'm working in Atlanta.
    A: In Atlanta? I've never been to the southern US. Are there many cultural differences between North and South?
2   A: Your firm specializes in manufacturing steel, doesn't it?
    B: Well, actually it used to. Now we also offer distribution and recycling services.
    A: Recycling services? As a matter of fact, we're looking for a company to support us with our recycling.
3   A: But you are satisfied with Isabel's work, aren't you?
    B: Yes, I am. I hope we can move her into a management job within the next three years.
    A: That will certainly be possible – and necessary – if she keeps bringing in new clients.
4   A: Did you enjoy your business trip to Frankfurt last week?
    B: Yes, I did. I even bumped into some old acquaintances at the airport.
    A: Some old acquaintances? That's always fun. Anyone I know?

Exercise 10

1   We don't have a formal chain of command.
2   It's important for our company strategy to be flexible.
3   We encourage our employees to expand their scope of responsibility.
4   Salaries are decided by both associates and supervisors.
5   Our product range includes components for the electronics industry.

Unit 2

Exercise 7

U = Ulrike, T = Tamara
U: Good morning, you must be Tamara.
T: Ulrike, good morning. It's a pleasure to meet you in person.
U: Nice to meet you, too. Did you have any trouble finding the restaurant?
T: None at all, thanks for asking. It is very conveniently located.
U: I guess we should try to order right away. Sometimes it gets very busy here.

T: Good idea. Do you have any suggestions?

U: Well, during business meetings I always order the English breakfast.

T: Sounds great. I'll have the English breakfast and a large black coffee.

U: So, have you been to Köln before?

T: No, this is my first visit. Well, this is the first visit during which I'll have time to look around.

U: It's great that the weather is a little warmer today.

T: Really? Well then, I'll have to consider myself lucky.

U: What are you planning to see while you're here?

T: I'm not sure. What do you recommend?

U: Well, I'd start by … Oh, here comes the waiter for our order.

6 Exercise 9

E = Erika, A = Arne

E: I have everything ready for the meeting with Fresh_Image. Is it true that this will be our first face-to-face contact with the web designer?

A: Yes. We've always communicated via email, but last month we had a big communication breakdown that resulted in a three-week delay. We want to avoid problems like that in the future.

E: I see. Are there any sources of possible conflict I should be aware of before the meeting?

A: No. I just think that sometimes people who work in different fields don't always communicate in the same way. In fact, I read an interesting article about that issue last month in a business magazine. A case study described how the differences can best be dealt with. Building mutual respect was one of the ideas given, and so I thought that I'd schedule a meeting so that we can increase our sensitivity toward each other.

E: Good idea. Your goal is to discuss the status of the different project milestones?

A: Exactly. I thought that would be a good place to start. Fresh_Image has excellent web designers. I hope we'll be able to work together on an ongoing basis.

Unit 3

7 Exercise 4

Jü = Jürgen, V = Vitale, D = Dana, Ja = Jan

Jü: So, hello – let's check that everyone's here. Vitale?

V: Yes, I'm here. Greetings from Italy.

Jü: Dana?

D: Good morning, everyone.

Jü: Jan?

Ja: Yes, I'm here. Hello from Prague.

Jü: So today we wanted to talk about a training provider for staff development. This is a point that you brought up in our last conference call, Dana.

D: That's right.

Jü: If we invest in a new help desk, we need to make sure that all staff are able to carry out their tasks.

Ja: Could you please speak more clearly? It sounds as if something's covering the phone.

Jü: Sorry, Jan. Of course. Is that better?

Ja: Yes, Jürgen, that's better, thanks.

Jü: The first point on the agenda is the topics that should be covered during the training. If you don't mind, I'd like to ask Vitale for his comments since he handled this in Italy.

V: Well, from my perspective there are three technical training aspects to consider: first, the point of sale equipment itself; second, handling the computer system so that the staff can access not only the email program to communicate with the customers but also all the technical documentation that's available; and third, the phone system so that the staff can handle the incoming calls effectively.

D: Sorry, Vitale, I didn't quite catch that. What was the third aspect? It sounds like someone's typing?

V: The phone system – taking the calls that come in and phoning the customers.

D: The phone system. Right. Thanks.

Jü: That seems like a good plan. What do the rest of you think?

Ja: Sounds fine to me.

D: Yes, it sounds good.

Jü: Okay, then, now we have a general overview of the topics that will be covered. In your experience, Vitale, how many days minimum should the training course last?

V: Well, ours was five full days, and it was very successful.

Ja: Could I just come in here? Do we have a budget for the training?

Jü: Good question, Jan. Actually no, not yet. We want to decide on the parameters first and then set the budget.

Ja: Oh, all right.

D: Sorry to interrupt, but I have a question for Vitale: were all staff members fully trained or just some of them?

Jü: Excuse me, but could I answer that one, Vitale?

V: Of course.

Jü: That's another good question. One thing we need to remember is that the help desk for Germany will be about twice the size as the one we set up in Italy. We have to assume that only the core staff – the assistant managers and full-time employees – will be trained, and they will be responsible for training the others.

D: Okay, well …

Ja: Vitale, would it be …

Ja: Excuse me, Dana, go ahead.

D: Sorry Jan, I was just going to say that the number of staff who are trained and whether they are responsible for training others will certainly be important for the way we need to look at this.

Jü: Absolutely.

Ja: Vitale, would it be possible for you to send us information about the training program that was held for your staff? Do you still have those records?

V: Yes, of course. And all the information is in English!

D: Um, Vitale, could I just ask you one more question? Is there anything that you would change if you had to plan the training again?

V: No, I don't think so. Of course it took the staff a while to get used to the new system, but we only had a few problems after the first two weeks. We were very pleased with the results of the training.

D: If I could cut in for a minute, Jürgen? I think that rather than continuing our conversation, maybe we should look at the documentation that Vitale sends. Then …

Exercise 5

Hi Rachel, this is Glen. It's 3 pm on Thursday. I hope your trip is going well and that your meetings have been successful. You asked me to give you a call and let you know the status of the optimization project. Well, we've received 15 offers and have evaluated them. We haven't made the final vendor selection, though, because we had to cancel yesterday's team meeting – Darin was out sick. So that means we haven't placed the orders either. We'll deal with both of those tasks tomorrow. We have managed to set the timeline, however. I'll send it to you in an email. See you next week. Bye.

Exercise 8 + 9

I = Interviewer, S = Stephanie, R = Ryan

1 **I:** Could you start by telling me a little about yourself?
 S: Well, I have five years of relevant experience. I am motivated, organized and have excellent communication skills.
 R: Sure. I'm 31 years old. I'm married and live in Soho. I have a bachelor's degree in business.

2 **I:** Why do you think I should hire you?
 S: Excellent question. I hope that you'll hire me because I'm the best candidate for the job.
 R: Why should you hire me? I think I'll be an excellent addition to your company. I think you're producing quality products, and I'm eager to be part of your success. My track record in winning customers speaks for itself. I have lots of energy, and I am a great team member to work with.

3 **I:** Would you mind telling me why you chose this career?
 S: Well, I chose it because it looked challenging. Every day is different. Plus, I enjoy working with people.
 R: Actually, my mother is in sales. She loves her job. I grew up seeing what she does, and so I decided to work in sales too.

4 **I:** How do you work under pressure?
 S: Oh, I don't have any problems working under pressure. None at all. The more pressure there is, the better I work.
 R: That's an interesting question. In sales you always have to stay cool. I think this is my biggest strength. If any kind of trouble comes up, I step back and give the customer some time. I'm honest. I don't get stressed out, and I never get annoyed, even if someone has made a mistake.

5 **I:** Can we look into the future for a moment? Where do you want to be in five years?
 S: Where do I want to be in five years? Honestly? I'd like to have your job. I know it sounds like an ambitious goal.
 R: In five years I hope that we'll be able to look back and see my contribution to the business – a steady increase in sales that is at least partly because of me. I'd like to be promoted to manager, but I'd also be happy as part of a team that works well together.

6 **I:** Would you mind telling me a little about your family situation? Do you have children?
 S: No, actually I don't, but are you really allowed to ask that in an interview?
 R: Yes, a boy and a girl. Gary and Sabrina. I have some pictures in my mobile if you'd like to see them.

Unit 4

Exercise 5

S = Ms Smith-Böhm, M = Ms Müller

S: Guten Tag, Smith-Böhm.
M: Hello, Ms Smith-Böhm? This is Susanna Müller from Personal Plus on Hauptstrasse. Did I reach you at a good time?
S: Oh – yes. Hello, Ms Müller. Now is fine.
M: Good. Ms Smith-Böhm, we've had an interesting assignment come in and we think you might be the right person for the job. The company is looking for someone who can work the early shift. Is that still possible for you?
S: Absolutely. I prefer working early in the day.
M: The company is located in the southeastern part of the city and needs someone to manage its warehouse while its usual manager is out sick. Most of the staff are foreign, but a few are German. As a result, English is essential, maybe even more important than German.

S: Let me make sure that I've understood you correctly. A company in the southeastern part of the city is looking for a first-shift warehouse manager?

M: Yes, that's right.

S: What does the company deal with?

M: The company produces plastic components for cars.

S: Oh, that does sound interesting. When would the job begin?

M: Well, they need someone as soon as possible. When could you start?

S: Next week would work. Let's say Monday?

M: Sounds good. I'll let the company know.

S: Just to summarize: The company manufactures plastic components for cars; most of the staff are foreign, so English is very important; and I'll start on Monday.

M: Yes, that's right. I'll email the complete details and the contract in a few minutes.

S: Great, Ms Müller. Thank you for thinking of me.

M: I'm glad it worked out. We hope this assignment is a good match for you, Ms Smith-Böhm. According to the company, the current manager is quite sick and might not return, so it might be a long-term opportunity for you.

S: That's good to know. Even though I like working with different companies, it would be nice to have a permanent position.

M: Well, we'll see what happens.

S: Right. I'll look forward to your email. Thanks again.

M: Goodbye.

S: Bye.

11 Exercise 7

H = Harshad, P = Patricia, B = Bill

H: Hello? This is Harshad. Is everyone on the line?

P: Hi, Harshad, this is Patricia in Dublin.

H: Hello, Patricia.

B: Good morning – this is Bill in Atlanta.

H: Hi, Bill. So, you both got the agenda?

P: Yes.

B: That's right.

H: Okay, so let's go ahead and start with the first point: improving the teamwork among the regions. We particularly need support right now in MENA, the Middle East and North Africa. My idea is to fly some colleagues from Europe and the Americas to the offices in MENA so that the employees can get to know each other and build what I hope will be long-term connections. What do you think?

B: Well, to be honest, I really disagree, Harshad. I think that we should develop some online interaction possibilities instead. I'm afraid that the personal contact could work against us. There would be a lot of cultural differences. And that could create a bigger problem than we have now.

P: I'm not so sure about that, Bill. I think it might be interesting if at least the team leaders met with employees at the smaller offices on-site. It might actually improve cultural understanding.

B: Well, that could be true. Let me think about it. By the way, Harshad, if we sent some staff over, who would pay for it?

H: That's a good question. This would come from the business development budget at headquarters, so you wouldn't need to worry about spending anything from your budgets.

B: How about we send over two or three team leaders from our offices in Europe and the Americas and combine it with a few video conferences? Then the visitors could introduce the MENA staff to the larger offices.

H: I'm not convinced that video conferences will work, Bill. But after the trips have been scheduled we can talk about that.

H: So, are we agreed that we should send a few team leaders from both Europe and the Americas to MENA in order to meet their colleagues in person?

B: Yes, I guess it can only improve the situation.

P: I think it's a good idea. I know my staff would look forward to it. Connecting a face with a name always improves communication.

H: Excellent. I know you're a little skeptical, Bill, but this is exactly what the business development consultants recommended.

H: Let's move on to the next point: recent orders. It seems that our orders have slowed down. I think we should launch an aggressive sales effort with our current clients to see if we can offer them services that are different from the ones that we already provide them.

B: Sounds good, Harshad. We're actually already planning something like this for the Americas. We're also looking for new clients, particularly companies that have recently entered the sector.

P: I'm sorry to disagree, but I don't think that will work in Europe. We probably need a different strategy. We already pitch other services to our clients and have several follow-up calls with them to make sure that we are offering them any services they might need.

H: Unfortunately I have to disagree, Patricia. A recent customer service survey in Europe found that most clients only contact us for the same services, not additional ones. In other words, we provide exactly the same services to exactly the same clients.

P: Really? I wasn't aware of that. Have the survey results been distributed?

H: No, actually not yet, but you should expect them next week.

P: Well, that changes things. Let me meet with my sales staff and team leaders. Could we come back to that issue in two weeks?

H: Sure, no problem. Is postponing our discussion OK with you, Bill?

B: It's all right with me. Meanwhile, I'll move forward with my staff as planned.

H: Good. That brings us to our last agenda item: updating the online order system.

Unit 5

🔊 12 **Exercise 2 + 4**

S = Sybille, J = Josef

S: Hello, Josef, it's good to see you again.

J: Thank you, Sybille, it's nice seeing you as well.

S: As my PA told you when setting up this appointment, I wanted to meet with you to talk about the project management job one more time. I think you know we were very impressed by your resume and qualifications.

J: Yes.

S: And we'd like to offer you the job.

J: That's great to hear. Thank you.

S: However, I think we have to talk a little bit about the terms, particularly the start date and the annual salary.

J: Alright.

S: Josef, it seems that we're running into a bit of a time problem. The current project manager leaves in three weeks, and we're behind schedule on two of her major projects. We think it's important that the new project manager, who we hope will be you, have a week or two here at the same time as the current project manager, so that she can hand over the projects and we don't lose any more time.

J: OK.

S: So that means that we'll offer you a bonus if you start the new position in two weeks instead of the usual four or eight weeks.

J: What kind of bonus were you thinking of?

S: Well, these projects are very important to our company and we know that if we don't do top work, our reputation will be negatively affected. This particular client has been known to "shop around" in a very obvious way. For example, if the client is dissatisfied with our work, when they distribute the invitations to tender for the next job, they will make it very clear that they worked with us in the past and will also tell other companies in their field about the problems they experienced with us. We can't afford to have any negative mark on our record.

J: I see.

S: If you start in two weeks instead of the usual four, we'll give you a 20 per cent bonus in addition to your first year's salary.

J: Hmmm. That's a very surprising offer.

S: Well, it's that important to us.

J: Of course that leaves me in somewhat of a difficult situation. I enjoy my current job and the company has been very good to me. I don't want to burn any bridges with them – not that I expect to return there, but only because our work relationship has been very good.

S: It's up to you, of course.

J: If I don't accept your offer to begin in two weeks, will you change your decision about offering me the job?

S: Honestly, we're not sure. You are one of two top applicants. We would like to hire you. But – through no fault of yours – you can see the situation we're in as well.

J: I assume that the yearly salary matches what was listed in the job ad?

S: Yes, it does, and …

🔊 13 Exercise 6

Good morning, ladies and gentlemen. My name is Enrico Rodriguez, and I'm the client relations manager at Worthington International. Thank you for inviting me here today to talk about the financial services we're able to offer your company. On average, Worthington International has helped companies improve their financial performance by between 5 and 7 per cent. As members of the finance committee, I'm sure you're interested in learning how we can help your company do the same! Today I'm going to discuss three main points. First of all, I'll tell you about our bookkeeping and payroll services; then I'll move on to our auditing services; and finally, I'll tell you a little bit about our investment management services. My talk will last about 15 minutes, and I'd be happy to take your questions after the presentation. So let's start with my first point, our bookkeeping and payroll services.

🔊 14 Exercise 8

1 Today I've informed you about our new employee bonus scheme. First I showed you how to track your performance using the intranet over the course of the year. Then I illustrated the direct link between your productivity and the bonus awards. Finally, I showed you the form that you and your supervisor must complete together in order for you to apply for a bonus. What does the new scheme mean for you? If you …

2 To conclude, let me just review the main points. First I showed that our technicians are well qualified and professional. Then I informed you about when they can be reached: they are available online 24/7. If they can't solve a problem online, they'll schedule a field visit. Finally, I explained how our annual preventative checks save companies thousands each year. In other words, if you …

3 I hope that my presentation has given you some idea of why you should choose electric cars for your company. As I explained during the presentation, electric cars are economical, energy efficient and environmentally friendly. I've also shown that because they look great on the road and attract people's attention, they bring your company positive PR – exactly what every company wants. So, by …

4   That brings me to the end of my presentation today. I've explained that the new business park at 348 Riley Avenue is close to all major roads and an international airport, is newly constructed using state-of-the-art energy technologies and has a flexible floor plan so that you can design the space you need for your company in any way that you wish. In sum, if you …

Unit 6

15   **Exercise 2**
1   That leads me to my next point. The line graph I'm going to show you illustrates the sales of two of our leading products during the last six months. The reason we're comparing them in this way is because we'd like to show you that their developments are surprisingly not comparable. Since you're all members of the marketing department we'd like to ask you to help us figure out why the two products – which are related – have such different sales trends. Now here's the graphic. The black line shows the development of the sales of OfficePro, and the green line shows the development of TopPro. As you can see, during the first three months of the year, sales of OfficePro increased steadily but then dropped suddenly in Month 4. They remained at that low level for the next two months. In contrast, TopPro had very low sales for the first two months, but at the beginning of the third month began a slow but steady increase that continued through Month 6.
2   Now for the next point and a question for you: why have sales been so different for two related products? Let me show you what I mean. See how different the sales of OfficePro and TopPro have been over the past six months? During Months 1 through 3, the sales of OfficePro rose steadily but then decreased suddenly in Month 4. TopPro, on the other hand, had low sales during Months 1 and 2 but began a constant rise in Month 3. Now we need to figure out what the issue is.

16   **Exercise 8**
1   Can we come back to that later? I'm fairly certain the information I'll present in a few minutes will answer your question.
2   Sorry. I don't know the answer to that, but I will find out. Could you please see me immediately after the presentation so I can get your contact information? I'd be happy to send you the answer within the next week.
3   I see what you mean. Oh, that's a good question. That's a point I don't address in my presentation today, but we'll definitely need to consider it for our next meeting in six weeks.
4   I see what you mean. Oh, that's a good question. Well, we thought that our efforts to increase production would also increase our efficiency. Unfortunately, that's not what happened.
5   Oh, that's a good question. If I understand you correctly, you'd like to know why we've chosen to outsource our help desk. Well, we looked at different options …
6   Can we come back to that later? I'd like to say more about that when we discuss last year's expenses.

Unit 7

17   **Exercise 2**
R = Richard, O = Oksana
R: I know that it's an excellent offer, but I'm terribly sorry, it simply isn't possible.
O: And what would you be interested in at the moment?
R: Ideally we'd like 20,000 units at 1.35 Euro each.
O: I see. Might you also be open to a slightly different proposal? What about 30,000 units at 1.30 each?

R: Your offer of 1.30 per unit is appealing, but I'm afraid we can't consider such a large quantity at the moment. It's simply too high. I've been given strict orders – the quantity is non-negotiable – we can't go above 20,000 right now.

O: Well, I suppose things may change.

Exercise 9

R = Roger, S = Simon

R: Hi, Simon, good to see you again.

S: Likewise, Roger. Thanks for coming in.

R: So, your assistant told me that you'd like to expand your corporate car fleet with some electric-powered cars?

S: Yes, that's right.

R: What exactly are you looking for?

S: Well, we recently hired 10 new employees. They'll all be on the road quite a bit. We were thinking that we would need at least five additional cars. We were thinking of using electric-powered cars, since we're promoting ourselves as a green company. And cost savings are a major consideration, as the price of gas keeps going up. Do you think we could work something out?

R: Absolutely. Let me just do a quick calculation – right. We could offer you five electric cars for 25,000 Euro each.

S: Wow. That's quite a bit higher than we expected. I assume that price includes the batteries?

R: Yes, it includes the original batteries and a three-year warrantee. What price do you have in mind?

S: I've done some research and we were hoping for something closer to 18,000 Euro per car.

R: We really couldn't agree to that at the moment. Maybe I could put forward another idea?

S: Of course.

R: Your main objective is to supply your new employees with electric cars, right?

S: That's right.

R: Well, the break-even point for electric cars can be as high as 10 to 15 years. Of course it makes sense that you'd like to protect the environment and improve your company's image, but I'm afraid that economically speaking, electric-powered cars are not the way to go at the moment.

S: I see your point. So what do you propose?

R: Well, suppose we were to offer you three electric cars at 25,000 Euro each, and two conventional cars with excellent fuel efficiency at 19,000 Euro each?

S: That's an interesting offer. But the decision for us to switch to electric-powered cars was a board decision – I don't have the authority to change it. But I might be able to argue for one conventional car for 18,000 Euro if you were willing to sell us four electric cars for 19,000 Euro.

R: Simon, to be honest, I really can't do that – the profit margin is simply too low for us. But how about 22,000 Euro for each electric car and 18,000 Euro for the conventional car?

S: Mmm, no, sorry. I simply wouldn't be able to explain to the guys in finance why we've gone so far over budget. You know you've been our exclusive supplier for over 10 years, but with those prices they'll ask me to get bids from other suppliers. Can't we reach some kind of compromise?

R: Yes, as you pointed out, your business is very important to us. Hm. Okay, then, what about one conventional car for 18,000 Euro and four electric cars for 21,000 Euro per car? Does that sound agreeable?

S: But one more thing – could you give us five-year warrantees instead of three-year warrantees on the electric-powered cars?

R: Absolutely.
S: Sounds like we have a deal. Thanks, Roger.
R: My pleasure.

Unit 8

19 **Exercise 4**

J = Simone Juarez, M = Hans Meyer

J: Thanks so much for sitting down with me today.

M: No problem. I was happy to hear that you're planning to write an article about our company for The Market Street News. As a company that's just starting out in the US, we're always eager for press.

J: Yes, well, we always try to keep an eye out for new companies and offices in the region. To start out, I'd like to check the most important details. Could I just confirm that your name's Hans Meyer?

M: Yes, that's correct. Meyer: that's M-E-Y-E-R.

J: M-E-Y-E-R. And your title is East Coast Regional Manager?

M: Yes, that's right. But that's funny, because at the moment our office is the only one in the US – oh, could you please not print that? Actually, by the end of next year we hope to open two additional offices – one on the West Coast and one in the Midwest.

J: No problem, Mr Meyer. I'll include that you're planning to open two additional offices, but I won't draw attention to your title. Excuse me just for a moment – I'm sorry to do this, but I'm afraid I have a little bit of a cold, so I'd like to take something so my voice lasts for the entire interview. Would you mind if I threw this in your trash can?

M: Well, actually in our offices we have a separate container for plastics. It's right behind you. Did you know that that little piece of plastic can be recycled?

J: No, actually I didn't.

M: I imagine we'll talk about that later on.

J: Yes. So, now for my questions. Why did your company decide to set up a branch here?

M: Do you mean in Massachusetts or the US in general?

J: The US in general.

M: Well, we believe that the waste disposal industry in the US market is growing and is still open to new competitors. We've been in the business for fifteen years and have achieved great success in the German market and in the Western European market in general. Five years ago we decided to enter the Eastern European market and have been successful there as well.

J: And you supply machinery that's used in the production of plastic?

M: That's right.

J: There's been some debate about the future of plastic. We know that it's bad for the environment – some plastics take hundreds of years to break down or decompose. What concerns do you have that your technology will become outdated in favor of technology and materials that are more environmentally friendly?

M: That's an interesting question. Actually, we're not at all concerned. On the one hand, we believe that, for better or for worse, plastic will be around as long as we have access to the oil that's needed to produce it. On the other hand, the machinery we produce is specifically built to handle the reprocessing of plastic. In other words, our machines recycle used plastic so that it can be used again as new plastic material.

J: So do you see yourselves as part of the future of plastic?

M: Yes, I have to say that we do.

J: How did the idea develop?

M: Well, as you're probably aware, Germany has very high standards in regard to recycling. Other countries in both Western and Eastern Europe have also begun to adopt strict recycling plans and comprehensive strategies …

20

Exercise 7

M = Mr Meyer, T = Mr Thomas

M: It seems that we've almost run out of options. You know we'd be happy to do business with you. Can you suggest a solution?

T: Sure. I'd be happy to make a suggestion. But first I think I need to give you more background on the business environment we're facing right now. When we sat down this afternoon, you probably didn't realize that my company has been trying to deal with incredible financial pressure. The board of directors is insisting that we trim the fat from all areas of our operation. That means that our operation budget has actually decreased from last year and doesn't even account for any type of inflation.

M: So you're saying that you won't be making any investments this year?

T: Not exactly. Perhaps it would be a good idea to consider long-term rental agreements – leases – for these machines.

M: I understand your position. I understand your concern. From your perspective, leasing the machines might be the only way for you to upgrade your current facilities?

T: Yes, that's right. But I'm afraid there's another issue. It seems that due to the financial crises, many small towns and cities are cutting back their recycling efforts. For example, instead of the small towns and cities collecting recyclable materials at every house, they are requiring people to go to designated locations to drop off the used materials. We think only people who are very concerned about the environment will do this. As a result, we expect the demand for our services – and our current facilities – to decrease within the next 12 months.

M: I understand your position. I understand your concern, and I really appreciate your openness about your current business situation. However, it seems to me that given all these financial pressures you'll have to improve your efficiency just to break even and stay in the market. How about doing something different? Maybe we could look into a lease-to-own arrangement?

Unit 9

21

Exercise 1

H = Host, B = Bernd

H: Today on Environmental Earth, we're pleased to have a representative from Aweco AG, Bernd Reimann, talk with us about the use of ultraviolet light for disinfecting water supplies. Thanks for being here today, Bernd.

B: Thanks for inviting me.

H: First, could you tell us a little bit about your company?

B: Sure. We manufacture large-scale water disinfection systems. That's our core business. We deal exclusively with ultraviolet light, or UV as we call it in the industry.

H: And who are your key customers?

B: Well, we work with municipalities that are responsible for providing communities with clean drinking water.

H: So tell us a little bit about water disinfection using UV.

B: I think it's important to point out that municipalities have traditionally disinfected their water using chemicals, such as chlorine. Chlorine is the same chemical that you'd use in a swimming pool – or in your laundry to make your clothing white. The chlorine that's used to disinfect water stays in the water. So imagine drinking that, even in low quantities! Our key process, which uses UV, kills microorganisms and is more environmentally friendly than using chemicals.

H: Is your method effective in every scenario?

B: No, unfortunately not. The process is most effective with certain types of small microorganisms. If the microorganisms are too large, then UV disinfection is used in combination with another method, such as a filter. Otherwise another process for disinfection has to be chosen.

🎧22 **Exercise 10**

P = Patrizia, G = Gerald

P: Oh, Gerald, I'm glad I ran into you. I wanted to ask you if you could help me out with something.

G: What's up?

P: Well, you know I'm headed to Brazil next week, and I have a mountain of work to do before I leave. I know how much you enjoy developing sales projections for the upcoming sales quarters – and every time you've stepped in for me in the past you've done an excellent job – so do you think you could work on the sales projections?

G: Sure, Patrizia, I'd be happy to. You're right – I really enjoy handling that.

P: That would be great! Thanks a ton. You're really helping me out. This trip to Brazil has required a lot more preparation than I thought it would.

G: Just to confirm, though, you need me to work on the sales projections for each car line?

P: No, no, sorry. Only the two luxury car lines.

G: Okay. Only the two luxury lines. And by when do you need them?

P: Oh, it has some time. Two weeks?

G: No problem. I'll get right on it. Let me know if there's anything else that comes up. And good luck with the final preparations for your trip.

P: I think that's it – unless you can teach me how to negotiate with Brazilian business people?

G: Uh, sorry. I think I'll stick with my sales projections.

Unit 10

🎧23 **Exercise 2**

L = Ling, R = Richard

L: Hello Richard? Ling Chen from Orania here.

R: Hello, Ling, how are things in Zurich?

L: It's just gorgeous out today, thanks. Lots of sun.

R: That's good to hear. It's been raining all day here.

L: Oh, that's too bad. Say, Richard, I have a few quick questions about the perfume bottles you're going to provide for our free samples. Our order was for 20,000 bottles. They'll hold 2 ml, right?

R: Let me just get my file. Yes, I got the order from Sam last week. 20,000 bottles. 2 ml.

L: And the colour of the bottles is going to be light blue, right?

R: Yes. Blue 508 on our chart – in other words, light blue.

L: Okay. And they'll be delivered in three weeks?

R: That's right.

L: Great, Richard, thanks so much.

R: No problem.

L: Bye.

R: Bye.

L = Liz, J = Jerry, M = Michele, W = Walt, D = Denise, H = Harrold

L: Thanks so much for coming, everyone. I hope you've each gotten some coffee and something to eat. I know that 7 am is early for most of you, so how about I briefly recap today's aim and see what ideas flow from there? In ten months we're going to launch our first-ever organic soap. We'd like to sell it in organic food markets and stores where natural products, such as clothing, are sold. So, in our focus group today, we'd like to explore the best way we can promote our product in advance. Every idea is open for discussion, so please don't hold back.

J: What about advertising in the store's weekly product brochure?

L Okay, that's a good start. Do all of you usually look through brochures from stores?

J: Every week.

M: Not really. If I do, I always want to buy more.

W: Yes I do, actually.

D: Absolutely. I love seeing what new products are available.

H: No, I don't have time.

L: Hmm. Looks as if even among us, the opinion is split. But let's keep it in mind, shall we?

D: Well, before the launch we could offer some kind of freebie – you know, a small sample of the soap. Something that people could take home with them when they leave the store.

L: Mmm. Interesting idea.

H: I have to say, I don't often shop at organic markets. In fact, I'm not quite sure how I got selected for this internal focus group, but when I do happen to go to an organic store I think that the best part is the free sample stands where you can try a small sample of the different foods. But unfortunately you can't try soap in a store.

L: Hmm. Wait a minute – why not? Sure, it would be more expensive to create a sample stand with running water, but I'm sure it's not impossible.

H: So you think that we could set up a stand with running water, like with a sink or something, and give the store's customers the opportunity to wash their hands?

L: Sure. Why not?

D: You know, I really like that idea. And I just thought of another one – what about online promotions?

L: Are you talking about emails to potential customers? Well, to be honest, I'm not so eager to do that. A few years back we ran into some trouble because our emails were considered spam.

D: No, actually I'm talking about forming an online group on a social networking site, or joining a group that already exists specifically for people who are careful about what products they buy.

J: Great idea.

L: Oh, yes, that's a very good suggestion. I wouldn't have thought of that. Do you think there would be any drawbacks?

D: Well, we'd have to be very careful about what we posted online. Different websites have different policies in regard to advertising and product promotion. We might need to be creative and hold an event that we only post a notice about through an online group.

W: Has anyone suggested direct mail yet? Could we buy some mailing lists and send a special flyer or coupon directly to members of our target groups?

L: Could you elaborate on that a bit?

W: Sure. I'd send mail to individual potential buyers and include an introduction to our company – especially explaining that we're trying to "go green", which is one of our corporate goals anyway. Then we can say that we're proud to introduce our first fully green product: organic soap.

L: Interesting idea. Maybe we could combine a few of the ideas that you've all brought up.

Audio-CD – Track list

1	Copyright	00:47
Unit 1		
2	ex. 1	01:27
3	ex. 4	01:15
4	ex. 10	01:42
Unit 2		
5	ex. 7	01:17
6	ex. 9	01:16
Unit 3		
7	ex. 4	03:48
8	ex. 5	00:47
9	ex. 8 + 9	02:49
Unit 4		
10	ex. 5	02:18
11	ex. 7	03:59
Unit 5		
12	ex. 2 + 4	02:52
13	ex .6	01:23
14	ex. 8	02:17
Unit 6		
15	ex. 2	01:46
16	ex. 8	01:37
Unit 7		
17	ex. 2	00:49
18	ex. 9	03:29
Unit 8		
19	ex. 4	03:25
20	ex. 7	02:18
Unit 9		
21	ex. 1	01:55
22	ex. 10	01:25
Unit 10		
23	ex. 2	01:08
24	ex. 7 + 8	04:02
Total running time		**48:41**

Studio: Clarity Studio Berlin

Tontechnik: Christian Marx, Pascal Thinius

Regie: Christian Schmitz

Sprecher/innen: Shaunessy Ashdown, Noémi Besedes, Steve Ellery, Mala Ghedia, Daniel Godor, Andreas Goebel, Marianne Graffam, Merlene Griffin, Manon Kahle, Pierpaolo de Luca, Murdo MacPhail, Peter Merrick, Justin Reddig, Darren Smith, Ian H. Smith, Kenneth Spiteri, Clare Wigfall